About This Book

Why is this topic important?

The odds of achieving organizational success after a merger or acquisition are not good. Research into the success of thousands of mergers and acquisitions—large and small—over the last twenty years shows that between 55 percent and 77 percent fail to deliver on their intended financial results. Most acquiring firms actually lose money on the acquisition.

The research also shows that this is primarily due to the failure to effectively assess and integrate the cultures of the companies involved in the merger or acquisition. The high failure rate and significant cost of failure are of increasing concern to the stakeholders of the companies involved—and not just the boards of directors and executives who make the deal, but the shareholders, employees, customers, suppliers, and community residents as well.

What can you achieve with this book?

This book makes a strong case for cultural due diligence, assessment, and integration planning as a major component of the merger and acquisition process and the resulting success of the merger or acquisition. While it speaks directly to the "deal makers"—the board, executives, and senior management—it is also a provocative and informative over-the-shoulder read for all stakeholders with a vested interest in the success of a merger or acquisition and the fate of the new company created by it.

The book details the cultural due diligence, assessment, and integration processes step by step and is a source of information that will enable the stakeholders of both companies to ask informed questions throughout the process and before it is too late. The examples, guidelines, and tools provided in the appendices and on the accompanying CD provide specific guidance for conducting cultural due diligence, assessment, and integration.

How is this book organized?

The book is organized into three parts. Part 1 deals with mergers, acquisitions, and organizational effectiveness. It summarizes the research on the failure rate of mergers and acquisitions and the high cost of failure, examining the organization as a complex system and presenting a model of organizational alignment as a key element of cultural integration. Part 2 focuses on the concepts, process, and procedures of cultural due diligence and assessment. Part 3 focuses on the concepts, processes, and procedures of cultural alignment and integration. The extensive Appendices provide examples, samples, and tools referenced in the book. The CD accompanying the book presents step-by-step guidelines and tools for performing cultural due diligence, assessment, and integration and PowerPoint summaries of the book's chapters for use in review or presentation to others.

Achieving Post-Merger Success

Achieving Post-Merger Success

A Stakeholder's Guide to Cultural Due Diligence, Assessment, and Integration

J. Robert Carleton
and
Claude S. Lineberry

Pfeiffer

A Wiley Imprint
www.pfeiffer.com

Printed in the United States of America

ISBN: 0-7879-6490-5

Library of Congress Cataloging-in-Publication Data

Carleton, J. Robert
Achieving post-merger success: a stakeholder's guide to cultural due diligence, assessment, and integration / J. Robert Carleton, Claude S. Lineberry.
    p. cm.
Includes bibliographical references and index.
  ISBN 0-7879-6490-5 (alk. paper)
  1. Consolidation and merger of corporations. 2. Corporate culture.
I. Lineberry, Claude S. II. Title.
  HD2746.5.C358 2004
    658.1′62—dc22   2003018519

Acquiring Editor: *Matthew Davis*
Director of Development: *Kathleen Dolan Davies*
Editor: *Rebecca Taff*
Senior Production Editor: *Dawn Kilgore*
Manufacturing Supervisor: *Bill Matherly*
Printed in the United States of America
Printing 10 9 8 7 6 5 4 3 2 1

Contents

List of Figures, Exhibits, and Worksheets

Contents of the CD-ROM

PowerPoint™ Slides

Section and Chapter Summaries

CDD/Integration Toolkit

CDD, Assessment, and Integration Process Flow Charts

The British Airways Transformation: A Systemic Approach

Dealing With National and Ethnic Culture Issues

Organizational System Scan Model

Organizational Scan Model: Methods and Uses

Organizational Scan Data Gathering Probes

Organizational Scan Survey

Nine-Step Alignment and Integration Model

Organizational Model

Organizational Alignment Initiatives Map

Traditional General Due Diligence Checklist

CDD Checklist

CDD High Level: Sample Key Person Interview

Acknowledgments

THE PRIMARY ACKNOWLEDGMENT that needs to be made is to the numerous researchers, practitioners, and academics who have gone before and laid the groundwork that made this addition to the understanding of organizations and human behavior possible. Many of these people are listed in the References at the end of the book. There are, however, a few people who merit special acknowledgement for their importance to the development of this book.

First and foremost among these is Dr. Donald T. Tosti. Don is a colleague, business partner on several occasions, and always close friend, whose fingerprints are identifiable throughout this book. In particular, the underpinning models of alignment and the organizational system that are the conceptual basis for Cultural Due Diligence and Cultural Integration have been shaped and refined over the years with Don's thought and input.

Another is Cathleen Hutchison, whose support and encouragement as a partner and colleague during the early development of these overall concepts was very important to the initial articulation of this area of organizational dynamics. Her intellectual probing, questioning, and polite yet insistent pushing kept me going in the early days in capturing and organizing the thoughts and activities that made the eventual detailing of this body of knowledge possible.

The last is probably breaking some sort of written or unwritten propriety, but I have to acknowledge the person with the most direct and critical impact on my ability to even contemplate writing this book, as well as my actually getting it done—my business partner, friend, colleague, and honored advisor in life and business, who is also the co-author, Claude S. Lineberry. Without his constant support, encouragement, and Herculean efforts, start to finish, this book would never have become a reality.

J. Robert Carleton
Conifer, Colorado

MY PRIMARY ACKNOWLEDGMENT is of the anonymous millions around the globe who get up and go to work each day, striving to do a good job in spite of the organizational turmoil and turbulence that swirls around them as the result of poorly planned and executed organizational change. Thanks to them for persevering and even finding humor in the chaos. Dilbert is indeed alive and well.

I'd to make special acknowledgement of my father, Claude S. Lineberry, Sr., the world's most logical and systematic man, from whom I have learned so very much—most of it unknowingly. Thanks Dad.

I would also like to offer special acknowledgement of Dr. W. Warner Burke, who opened my eyes to the world of organizational dynamics and systems, patiently answered my at times naïve questions, and had faith in me when it counted. He also showed me that a boy from Alabama can indeed succeed in the strange world of high-stakes consulting.

Certainly my wife Mari and son Michael merit acknowledgment just for putting up with me generally, and especially over the months that this book was in development. I also acknowledge and welcome my first grandson, Alexander Charles Geczy, who brings me great joy and will receive the first autographed copy of this book—much to the envy of his play group pals.

And finally, special acknowledgment to my co-author, partner, colleague, and friend, Bob Carleton, who really did the heavy lifting in the development of this book. Without his clear thinking and his at times voluminous and stream-of-consciousness input, this would be a thin tome indeed.

Claude S. Lineberry
Eagle Lake, California

Preface

THE BRIEF ARTICLE, written in 1997, that evolved into this book started as a frustrated howl at the moon about the insanity of many post-merger situations and the chaos and costs resulting from what we had come to consider nothing more than bad or shortsighted planning.

We had just completed yet another post-merger "triage" project for a client who had, a year earlier, expanded into an otherwise closed market by acquiring a major competitor. In spite of the business logic and business promise of this acquisition, one year later service and quality standards in the acquired operation were far below its pre-acquisition levels—and steadily getting worse. We were asked to get-involved and to see whether anything could be salvaged or if the acquisition should be divested and written off.

We had been in these situations before with other clients—after a heralded acquisition showing great promise on paper, the post-merger or acquisition period often saw operational performance worsen. Often disagreement and dissatisfaction on the part of both customers and staff increased, service and quality levels diminished, staff/management relations worsened, and revenues declined. In short, the great promise of the acquisition or merger was not being realized.

In these cases, we were generally able to resolve the issues and help the organization move toward achieving the originally intended results through intensive intervention into the overall organizational system and by making adjustments to the organizational culture. Our frustration stemmed from our success in improving the situation—after the fact. If we could do this successfully in different companies reactively, how much easier would it be to proactively avoid these post merger and acquisition problems in the first place?

This set us off on several years of extensive research on mergers and acquisitions, and especially on their success or failure. That, coupled with our continuing experience in helping clients deal with post merger or acquisition problems, resulted in this book. The intent of this book: to make it possible for organizations to achieve post-merger success in a timely manner.

We hold strong views about the obligations of management and the fiduciary responsibility of executives to the organizations' stakeholders when they choose to engage in a merger or acquisition. The current merger and acquisition (M&A) track record is not good, and the stakeholders—especially the shareholders—are taking the brunt of the resulting losses. We hope that any stakeholder of an organization—shareholder, employee, customer, or supplier—who has a vested interest in the success of the organization can utilize the information in this book to ascertain the adequacy of due diligence and forward planning performed in conjunction with a merger or acquisition. We sincerely hope that this book will be a force for improving the success of mergers and acquisitions, thereby making life better and a bit less traumatic and uncertain for the organization's stakeholders—especially the organization's staff and management.

Introduction

"Of course the merger was a success. Neither company could have lost that much money on its own."

Steve Case, Former Chairman of the Board,
AOL/Time Warner

THE ODDS OF ACHIEVING organizational success after a merger or acquisition are not good—no matter whether the companies involved are small, with a few million in annual sales and a few hundred employees, or whether they are corporate giants, with billions in annual sales and thousands of employees around the world. The complexity of mergers and acquisitions certainly increases with the size of the companies involved, but large or small, most mergers and acquisitions fail for the same two basic reasons: (1) failure to assess the potential impact of attempting to merge and integrate the cultures of the companies involved and (2) failure to plan for systemic and systematic and efficient integration of those cultures.

The high failure rate of mergers and acquisitions and the significant costs related to failure are an increasing concern to the stakeholders of both companies involved—obviously their Boards of Directors, CEOs, executive teams, and management, but also their shareholders, employees, customers, suppliers, and residents of the communities in which they do business.

While this book speaks directly to the deal makers at the Board, executive, and senior management levels, it is also intended as a provocative and informative "over the shoulder" read for all stakeholders with a vested interest in the success of a merger or acquisition and in the fate of the new company created by it. By presenting the data and research findings from mergers and acquisitions over the last fifteen years, and by identifying the key issues related to assessment of cultural dynamics and the planning of cultural integration, we intend this book to be a source of informed tough questions that should be asked early in the merger or acquisition, before it is too late to respond with the answers. In our practice, we use the Cultural Assessment and Integration Flowchart shown in Figure I.1 as a blueprint and the means for discussing cultural assessment and integration within an organization. The flowchart shows all the steps that we use as we consult to merging organizations.

The processes for *cultural assessment* and *cultural integration* presented here are the result of several years of research into the success or failure of mergers and acquisitions in companies of all sizes, in all industries, and involving domestic, international, and global companies, as well as our involvement as consultants in a number of mergers, acquisitions, and strategic alliances over the last fifteen years. While our focus in this book is on mergers and integrations, the processes described here are also appropriate when considering possible strategic alliances, joint ventures, partnerships, and other types of organizational collaboration.

We intend the book to be a "how to" guide to achieving post-merger success through attention to cultural assessment and cultural integration planning at the conceptual and tactical level, detailing what to do, in what sequence, and why. It is not a prescriptive step-by-step guide. In something as complex as the assessment and integration of organizational culture, how these two critical activities are accomplished must be determined by the organization involved, based on its own unique characteristics. Throughout the book and on the CD that accompanies it, numerous operational-level tools, checklists, worksheets, and samples are presented as "how to" resources. The book is organized into three parts:

- Part 1: Mergers, Acquisitions, and Organizational Effectiveness
- Part 2: Cultural Due Diligence and Assessment
- Part 3: Cultural Alignment and Integration

Figure I.1.   Cultural Due Diligence, Assessment, and Integration Flowchart

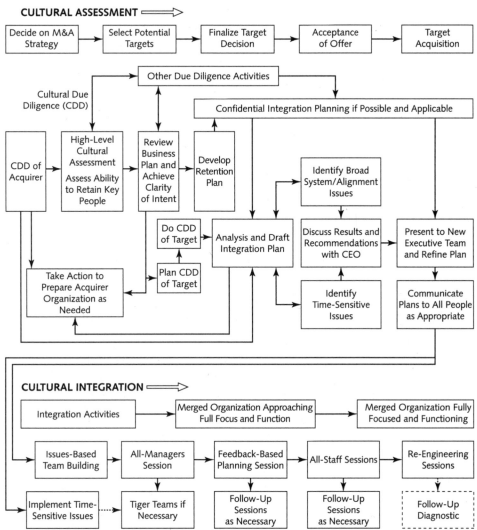

Achieving Post-Merger Success. Copyright © 2004 by John Wiley & Sons, Inc. Reproduced by permission of Pfeiffer, an Imprint of Wiley. www.pfeiffer.com

The accompanying CD presents a summary of the key concepts of each chapter and a library of operational-level tools, samples, and information.

Mergers, Acquisitions, and Organizational Effectiveness

PART 1 OF THIS BOOK consists of three chapters:

- Chapter 1: Mergers, Acquisitions, and Organizational Culture
- Chapter 2: The Organization as a System
- Chapter 3: Organizational System Alignment

In these chapters we present the data and research findings on the success of mergers and acquisitions, present the business case for cultural due diligence and assessment, define and discuss organizational culture and performance, and establish the prerequisite concepts and understanding required to deal with the details of *cultural assessment* and *cultural integration* presented in Parts 2 and 3 of the book.

Mergers, Acquisitions, and Organizational Culture

AFTER A RELATIVELY SHORT HIATUS following the infamous events of September 11, 2001, and their impact on the U.S. economy, the pace of mergers and acquisitions (M&A) around the globe is again on the rise—in spite of an abysmal financial track record to date for these deals. According to recent government statistics, a major increase in merger activity is already underway, based on what is anticipated to be a 300 percent increase in applications for antitrust clearance (required for mergers valued at more than $50 million). The $318 million in antitrust application fees so far in 2003 is the largest amount ever raised from the pre-merger notification program and represents some 2,800 mergers of over $50 million in value anticipated in 2004—more than twice the number of mergers reported to antitrust agencies in 2002.

Driving this wave of M&A activity is the desire by companies—large and small—all over the globe to gain competitive advantage through growth, consolidation, and entry into new markets. In order to do this, they must find and form some type of alliance, merge with or acquire partner companies offering strategic synergy. Such alliances can offer the combined companies economies of scope and scale, a more comprehensive product and services inventory, broader geography, access to new markets, and a solid platform for globalization.

The deals all look good on paper, but serious problems lurk in the process, as can be seen in their track record.

THE M&A REPORT CARD

The failure rate of mergers and acquisitions is unreasonable, unacceptable, and unnecessary. Clearly, mergers and acquisitions will continue to be the growth strategy of choice, as they were in the 1990s, which—with some notable exceptions—flies in the face of the marked lack of success of such deals to date. In a 1995 review of thirty years of activity, *Business Week* came to the conclusion that most of the time the acquirers actually *lose* money on the acquisition. In *The Art of M&A Integration* (Lajoux, 1998), fifteen studies are listed that were done between 1965 and 1997, covering well over seven thousand mergers and acquisitions in depth. The bottom line for these studies and many more is that between *55 and 77 percent* of all mergers fail to deliver on the financial promise announced when the merger was initiated.

Other disquieting evidence of difficulty with mergers and acquisitions:

- The *Business Week* study also showed that stock prices of acquiring companies fell an average of 4 percent and that there was generally a negative correlation between mergers and acquisitions and increased profitability.

- Typically there is a 50 percent dropoff in organizational productivity during the first four to eight months after the merger or acquisition.

- Stock price declines approximately 70 percent of the time on a company's announcement of a merger or acquisition.

- Only 23 percent of acquisitions earn back their capital cost.

- General Electric states that 95 percent of its acquisitions over the past decade yielded "disappointing results."

- A 1992 University of Chicago survey showed that almost half of the businesses acquired in mergers were later sold again, many times at a significant loss.

- A McKinsey Consulting study showed that, of 115 large acquisitions in the early 1990s, 60 percent were considered failures within five years.
- Studies show that some 40 percent of cross-border mergers among large companies end in what is termed "total failure," with the acquiring companies never recovering their capital investment.

Overall, the success of mergers and acquisitions over the last decade gets a grade of C- at best (Galpin, 2000).

M&A FAILURE COSTS

The cost of failure is significant. According to *Fortune* magazine, thirty years of M&A activity has resulted in an average of 3 percent loss of equity. Other direct "hard" failure costs include:

Lower Share Price

- Over the last three decades, almost 17.5 percent of merger acquiring firms lost more than 5 percent of their value upon announcement of the merger, while only 11 percent had corresponding positive returns (AMS, 2001).
- The average acquirer lost almost 4 percent of its value (3.8 percent) in the medium term as a result of the merger (Andrade, Mitchell, & Safford, 2001).
- In deals financed by the issuance of equity, acquiring firms lost over 6 percent of their value over the medium term as a result of the announced merger (Andrade, Mitchell, & Safford, 2001).
- A *Journal of Economic Perspectives report* (Andrade, Mitchell, & Safford, 2001) using a sample of mergers from 1961 through 1993, showed that, in the three years following the merger point, estimates of abnormal stock price reactions are quite negative: -5 percent for an equal-weighted portfolio of firms (-9 percent when the deal was financed with stock), and -1.4 percent for a value-weighted portfolio. In addition, growth firms underperform by an average of -6.5 percent equal-weighted and -7.2 percent value-weighted.

Excessive Acquisition Premiums

- Acquirers pay premiums that average as much as 25 percent (Andrade, Mitchell, & Safford, 2001, and many others), indicating that most if not all of the economic benefits of mergers accrue solely to the shareholders of the target firm and not to the acquirer owners.

Decreased Profitability

- Approximately 60 percent of mergers result in lowered profitability for as long as seven years post-merger, compared to a control group of non-merger firms (Schenk, 2000).

Changes in Productivity

- McGlickin and Nguyen (1995) report that, while industrial acquirer plants show increased productivity in the short run, acquirer plants endure longer term productivity losses. AMS (2001) and Schoar (2002) point out that the net productivity gain for mergers is thus zero on average.

Loss of Market Share

- Some research asserts that acquired firms involved in mergers lose 75 percent of their pre-merger market shares on average, compared to firms in the same industry that were not acquired (Mueller, 1986).

Bad Bidders Become Good Targets

- Stock price reactions of acquirer firms whose acquisitions were subsequently divested (likely failures) are reliably and strongly negative (about −4 percent of firm value) (Mitchell & Lane, 1990), indicating that the market often punishes firms for making bad or unsuccessful merger decisions.
- In addition, acquiring firms that are unsuccessful themselves become targets, and the market appears to sense this. Firms whose acquisitions result in divestitures and who subsequently become targets lose about 7 percent on average at the initial announced merger. About 40 percent of these bad bidders soon become acquisition targets themselves, according to Mitchell and Lane (1990).

Indirect "soft" costs of failure or ineffective integration are significant as well, and include:

Lack of External Focus on the Customer, Competition, and the Marketplace

- News of a merger or acquisition attracts attention and can prove unsettling to customers and the financial community. Competitors can take advantage of this turbulence and actively market and sell on the basis of it. At the precise time when strong external focus is essential, the acquiring and target company can become distracted by the complex internal issues of integration and fail to focus sufficiently on their external *stakeholders*.

Low Staff Motivation and Morale

- In most mergers and acquisitions, the rumor mill accurately runs months ahead of any formal corporate communication about a merger or acquisition. Meetings of executives between the two companies, visits by consultants, and requests for documentation are all evidence that something is going to happen. As staff hear the rumors and business news reports, speculation runs rampant in both companies. Absent any formal communication on the merger or acquisition about what will happen, why, when, and how, survey after survey indicates widespread anxiety, loss of motivation, and decreased morale—all with serious negative impact on performance and service levels.

Loss of Key Executives—Nearly Half Within Three Years

- One observable indicator of a pending merger or acquisition is the daily arrival—morning and afternoon—of the Federal Express truck delivering documentation from executive recruiters and picking up the completed documentation from key executives. Again, the news of a merger or acquisition creates a window of opportunity for competitors to take advantage of a period of uncertainty and to poach executive talent away from the acquiring or target company. Research indicates that up to half of the executives in firms involved in a merger or acquisition leave within three years (Galpin, 2000).

Loss of Key Staff—Many Long-Serving High Performers and Informal Leaders

- In times of organizational upheaval—as with a merger, acquisition, or other large-scale change—if communication about the change (specifically about staff reduction, reassignment, or relocation) is not handled well, the best and brightest leave first. Obviously, the more talented, technically competent, and experienced are the most in demand in the marketplace, and they find little difficulty in obtaining a new job—often with the competition and at significantly higher compensation. This can represent a serious "brain drain" in areas of technical expertise, with replacement being costly and time-consuming. The antidote to this problem is disclosure—as early and as full as possible—about the architecture of the merger or acquisition and the reasons behind it. This is especially true in the case of key staff, who should be helped to see clearly the new vision and strategy and the opportunities it represents for them in the new company.

Brand Confusion—Loss of Brand Focus

• Often in mergers and acquisitions, one of the brands goes away. In the case of the merger of Bank of America and Nations Bank, even though Nations was the acquiring company, the corporate brand became Bank of America because of its global brand recognition. When First Union and Wachovia merged, the decision was to operate through 2003 under both brand names, and then take on the strong Wachovia brand, even though First Union was the larger of the two organizations. First Union became the corporate brand except in certain areas like the securities business, where Wachovia had better brand recognition. With the Hewlett-Packard and Compaq merger, the new company assumed a new brand identity as *hp,* except for certain Compaq products well-known in the PC marketplace that continue to carry the Compaq brand. All of this can be very confusing and emotional, especially to the target company whose staff feel a real sense of loss of identity. Customers perceive this lack of brand focus and confusion as indicators that there is no real commitment to the merged operations, and again an advantage for competitors is created. The logic and business rationale of re-branding, selective branding, and product line consolidation should be made clear early in the communication process.

Decreased Customer Service Levels and Satisfaction

• All of these factors and more can contribute to significantly decreased levels of customer satisfaction. Integration problems, if not properly anticipated, can unintentionally put barriers in the path of customer service—as with conversion to a new telephone or e-mail system, consolidation of customer data bases, integration of billing systems, and so forth. All the customer knows is that telephone calls are not returned promptly, e-mail messages are kicked back, and billing errors are frequent and difficult to resolve. All too often, customer focus is lost due to a poorly planned and inefficient integration. No one is talking to the customer about the merger or acquisition prior to the fact about new customer benefits or checking with the customer during the integration process. Even key accounts are left unattended and vulnerable to the competition.

Given this dismal history, there have been numerous studies to ascertain why the merger and acquisition record is so poor. In *The Synergy Trap*, Mark Sirower, (1997) places part of the blame on the payment of excessive acquisition premiums for the alleged synergies that will be gained in the future by the new organization. He also points out that, above all, speed is of the essence in the merger and acquisition process, in that—given the value of money over time—time really is money. But while this excessive premium cost may well be a major factor, it is not the primary cause of the high failure rate.

WHY MERGERS AND ACQUISITIONS REALLY FAIL

In short, *culture clash,* the impact of operational and cultural problems stemming from cultural differences of the two organizations involved in the merger or acquisition , is undeniably the primary causal factor in the failure of mergers and acquisitions and strategic alliances.

Coopers and Lybrand, the British Institute of Management, Watson-Wyatt, and a long list of researchers have all come up with the same findings—*culture clash* results in internal confusion and in-fighting, characterized by different or unfamiliar ways of *"doing things and talking about things."* These in turn result in huge inefficiencies, loss of time, and increased internal focus at the exact same time that the new company needs absolute ringing clarity on purpose, plan, and action, with strong external focus.

What is culture clash? It is best defined by its symptoms:

- Observable differences between the companies involved in a merger about: *What is believed; what is important; what is valued; what should be measured; how people should be treated; how people treat one another; how decisions are made; how to manage and supervise; and how to communicate.*

- The disruption that occurs when the way one company conducts its business and treats its people is folded in with another company's way of doing business.

- Differences of opinion, disagreements, arguments, and different assumptions regarding the internal process of implementing the new business plan and strategy.

- Perceived differences in organizational beliefs, values, and practices.
- Perceived differences between the two companies in degree of formality in style of dress, language, work space, communication, and so forth.
- *"Winner-loser"* language used by either organization's people.

Since speed in implementing the integration and achieving post-merger effectiveness is absolutely critical, and culture clash is the biggest obstacle to achieving the clarity and focus necessary for rapid implementation, then what is generally being done to anticipate and manage culture and management style integration issues?

The general answer is *very little* or *nothing at all.* In their 1999 study of 190 CEOs and CFOs experienced in global acquisitions, Watson Wyatt found that cultural incompatibility is consistently rated as the greatest barrier to successful integration, but that research on cultural factors is least likely to be an aspect of due diligence. What a conundrum! The greatest barrier to success of a merger or acquisition is the least likely to be researched during the due diligence process.

Why does this situation exist? The answer seems to lie with the arrogance of CEOs, Boards, and senior management teams, who assume cultural compatibility of the two organizations in the absence of any due diligence, or strongly believe that even if culture clash does occur nothing can really be done about it. These assumptions persist in the face of a dismal M&A track record and significant research and literature on the impact of culture on M&A success. The result? Post-merger performance that looks like that shown in Figure 1.1.

Figure 1.1. Typical Post-Merger Performance

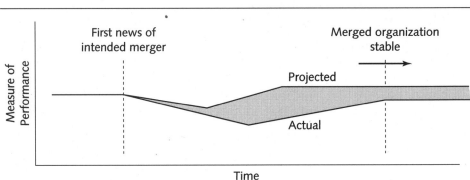

ORGANIZATIONAL CULTURE AND CULTURE CLASH

This kind of false assumptions about cultural compatibility and the inevitability of culture clash were clearly demonstrated at the Best of Mergers and Acquisitions Conference in Tampa, Florida, in 2000. Ten of the twelve speakers made it very clear that, while organizational culture was undoubtedly an area that was important to M&A success, they didn't feel it was possible to do much about it.

At a Conference Board seminar in New York in 2001, the majority of speakers said that culture was critical, but that it was impossible to deal with it in an effective and predictable manner. The collective wisdom seems to be that the cultural impact on a merger or acquisition and the inevitable culture clash issues that arise *just have to be lived through!*

In these post-Enron/WorldCom/TYCO times, when the individual and collective behavior of corporate Boards of Directors, CEOs, and the executive team is under increased and continuing scrutiny, does negligence stemming from arrogantly held positions and false assumptions about the impact of cultural compatibility on the success of mergers and acquisitions become malfeasance? The data are clear, research and examples abound, and there is a large body of knowledge on organizational culture, cultural due diligence, and cultural integration. Certainly senior HR executives, CFOs, and chief counsels are aware of this body of knowledge, as it is a frequent topic of discussion in their respective journals and professional societies.

Soon the shareholders of a company that is party to a mismanaged and failed merger or acquisition won't be willing to take their lumps silently. They can and will allege malfeasance on the part of the Board of Directors and executive team for overlooking the impact of cultural compatibility as part of the due diligence process.

A clear precedent can be found in a 1991 decision by the Delaware Chancery Court—the same court that dismissed Walter Hewlett's suit attempting to block the HP-Compaq merger in 2002. In the Time Warner versus Paramount suit, the court concluded: "Consistent with the general law, the moral issues must be decided pursuant to moral values that, in bid cases, include as one factor the internal culture of the target corporation and presumably also the host culture in which the corporation carries on business."

The assumption that corporate culture clash in M&A cannot effectively and reliably be managed is absolutely false. Corporate culture can be and has been managed very effectively in a number of companies over the years. Kotter and Heskett, in their book *Corporate Culture and Performance* (1992), demonstrated with painstaking research that corporate cultures are real, that they can be effectively managed, and that, if managed properly, they will also produce long-term economic performance that far outstrips the results of companies that do not manage their cultures.

A CASE STUDY IN MANAGING CULTURE—BRITISH AIRWAYS

From 1984 to 1994, British Airways under the leadership of Colin Marshall clearly demonstrated the ability to fundamentally change its longstanding and deeply embedded organizational culture in order to deliver dramatically improved results in terms of customer satisfaction, employee satisfaction, shareholder satisfaction, and profit—regardless of general overall trends in the airline industry. This culture shift is generally considered the first large-scale corporate transformation to have been successfully achieved.

During this period, British Airways acquired British Caledonian Airways and found itself in the midst of a full-blown culture clash, particularly within the Gatwick airport operations, where service levels and profits were plummeting while they were steadily improving at Heathrow. Once the cultural issues were focused on, this situation was turned around definitively in less than six months—even though resolution of culture clash after the fact takes far more time, effort, and resources to resolve than does cultural integration that is planned from the beginning of the merger or acquisition process. (More details are presented in Appendix A.)

THE PREVAILING WISDOM IS WRONG

A number of similar cases have been reported, both in terms of successful internal integration of culture/style within an existing company, as well as in part of an integration of merged company cultures—but it is still clearly the exception rather than the rule. The primary reason for this rests with the abundance of misinformation and misunderstanding about corporate cultures, how they are formed and managed, how they can be analyzed, and how they can be merged or modified.

Partly because of the fact that full understanding of the culture aspect of organizations is still developing, a problem exists with definitions and general understanding of what is meant by corporate culture. It is complicated because corporate culture has many components and in fact is only a manifestation of an overall system.

"Culture" cannot be dealt with in isolation; a simple and focused "culture change" program is almost assuredly going to fail to create sustainable, measurable change. To work with the culture of an organization is to work with all of the factors of the company that have any bearing on why people behave the way they do on the job from day to day. To effectively manage the organizational culture is to deal with hiring, firing, incentives and compensation, decision making, organizational structure, policies, procedures, technology, work flow, management and leadership styles, processes, and measures—at a bare minimum.

CULTURE AS THE CULPRIT

When we first began researching and writing on organizational culture (Lineberry & Carleton, 1992), there was still active debate as to whether or not corporate culture existed and, if it did, whether or not it had a significant impact on organizational performance. Over the intervening years, that debate has been resolved: it is now generally agreed that all organizations, irrespective of size, have a corporate culture and that its impact on organizational performance and results is enormous (Kotter & Heskett, 1992). The debate now focuses on how to best align the organization's strategy, culture, and supportive infrastructure to achieve and maintain competitive advantage in an increasingly turbulent global business environment. This is a significant priority because of the exponential increase in mergers, acquisitions, and strategic alliances as a strategy for corporate growth and industry consolidation into the millennium.

The importance of compatible cultures in mergers, acquisitions, and alliances has given rise to a need for cultural corporate due diligence (Carleton, 1997) as a consideration of equal or greater importance than the traditional financial and legal due diligence that typically precede such deals.

"Culture clash" is a term that appears frequently in the world's financial and business press, usually in explaining why the intended merger, acquisition, or alliance failed or was abandoned at the last minute by one or both parties.

Corporate culture has been clearly established as a major driver of organizational performance and results, and of individual performance within organizations. Over the past decade, the evolution and development of a technology for the analysis, assessment, and management of corporate culture has quickened. Culture and culture change are now common business terms, heard on the line and on the shop floor, not just in the Boardroom or HR department. The clear research-based business case for cultural due diligence in planning and executing mergers and acquisitions can no longer be ignored, neglected, or denied.

DEFINING ORGANIZATIONAL CULTURE

So what is this thing that has so captured the attention of managers, consultants, and now Wall Street and the world's financial markets? It certainly is not new; corporate or organizational culture, by definition, has been around for as long as organizations have. Various definitions of organizational culture have been reported by Schein (1985), among them the following:

- The norms that evolve in working groups, such as the particular norm of "a fair day's work for a fair day's pay" that evolved in the Bank Wiring Room in the Hawthorne studies (Homans, 1950);

- The feeling or climate that is conveyed in an organization by the physical layout and the way members of that organization interact with customers or other outsiders (Tagiuri & Litwin, 1968);

- The dominant values espoused by an organization, such as product quality or price leadership (Deal & Kennedy, 1982);

- The philosophy that guides an organization's policy toward employees and/or customers (Ouchi, 1981; Pascale & Athos, 1981); and

- The rules of the game for getting along in the organization; "the ropes" that a newcomer must learn to become an accepted member (Ritti & Funkhouser, 1982; Schein, 1968, 1978; Van Maanen, 1976, 1979)

All of these definitions touch on certain aspects of organizational culture, but none can be considered full and complete in itself. Schein (1985) provides a fuller and more essential definition of the term as "a pattern of basic assumptions—invented, discovered, or developed by a given group as it learns to cope with its problems of external adaptation and internal integration—that has worked well enough to be considered valid, and, therefore, to be taught to new members as the correct way to perceive, think and feel in relation to those problems." Or, in the tersely eloquent words of Burke and Litwin (1989), organizational culture is *"the way we do things around here."*

Many key organizational issues relating to effectiveness—quality, customer satisfaction, teamwork, innovation, decision making, and flexibility, to name a few—are primarily driven by the organization's culture. Therefore, organizational culture is a critical aspect of organizational survival and success, and the ability to analyze, understand, and manage the culture of the organizations that are merging is vital.

Whether dealing with an overall organizational culture or with a subculture, the term *managing the culture* can wrongly imply a much larger effort than is appropriate. It can conjure up notions of total creation, replacement, or transplantation of a culture, when what is intended is some modification of the existing culture—a change in the values/beliefs/behaviors system. Change efforts may be relatively small, as in altering a particular behavior pattern (using the customer's name in all telephone contacts), or relatively large, as in establishing a new value within the culture (continuous improvement or customer focus). The scope of the effort and its focus result from a systematic and empirical analysis of the organization and its culture(s).

No matter what the scope and focus of the intended culture change, it is wise to keep in mind the caution offered by O'Toole (1985): anthropology indicates that culture changes in one of two basic ways, revolution or evolution, and attempts at revolutionary culture change always fail; it is the shared experience and common history of a group over time that changes the culture.

CULTURE AND PERFORMANCE—THE HARD DATA

The impact of corporate culture on organizational performance and financial results is very real. As we have said, analysis and management of corporate culture is key to business success and can no longer be considered as corporate social work to be looked after solely by the HR department, if at all.

It is real business, as demonstrated by Kotter and Heskett (1992) in their long-term study of largest ten to eleven high-performing companies in each of twenty-two industries over a seventeen-year time period. The study included companies such as Hewlett-Packard, Xerox, Nissan, and First Chicago and a quantitative study of the relationship between culture and performance in more than two hundred companies. They reported that those companies that actively managed their cultures to be adaptive and flexible outperformed companies with strong but rigid cultures by an impressive margin, as shown below.

Adaptive Versus Non-Adaptive Culture Results*

- Revenue increase of 682 percent versus 166 percent
- Workforce expansion of 282 percent versus 36 percent
- Stock price increase of 901 percent versus 74 percent
- Net income increases of 756 percent versus 1 percent

They concluded that "the vast majority of firms currently do not have cultures that are sufficiently adaptive to produce excellent long-term economic performance." Clearly, managing the corporate culture is a significant activity in leading and managing the business—and it merits special focus in mergers and acquisitions.

NATIONAL VERSUS ORGANIZATIONAL CULTURE

Increasingly, mergers and acquisitions are done internationally, attempting to bring together two or more companies representing different national cultures, for example, Chrysler and Mercedes-Benz, Volkswagen and Rolls-Royce, British Petroleum and AMOCO, Groupe Schneider and Square D. Even without a merger, as companies globalize, they have operations in countries other than the company's home country. In any case, multiple national cultures introduce an additional complexity that must be considered when analyzing corporate cultures.

Although it is beyond the scope of this book to deal comprehensively with the special challenges and increased complexity that different national or ethnic cultures bring to a merger or acquisition, some basic points of consideration may prove helpful.

Stephen Rhinesmith, one of the world's leading researchers and strategists on globalization, relates an anecdote in *A Manager's Guide to Globalization* (1996) that provides a glimpse of the unique difficulties that can be part of cross-cultural

*From Kotter & Heskett (1992).

alliases: "Life can be tough on the frontier of globalization. Take the joint venture among three competing high tech companies from three continents—Siemens AG of Germany, Toshiba Corporation of Japan, and IBM. They are trying to develop a new chip together in East Fishkill, New York. The Triad, as they call themselves, are working in an IBM facility in the Hudson River Valley with over 100 scientists from the three organizations. Not surprisingly, cultural factors are a major challenge in the operation. *The Wall Street Journal* (May 3, 1994) reported:

> 'Siemens scientists were shocked to find Toshiba colleagues closing their eyes and seeming to sleep during meetings (a common practice for overworked Japanese managers when talk does not concern them). The Japanese, who normally work in big groups, found it painful to sit in small, individual offices and speak English; some now withdraw when they can into all-Japanese groups. The Americans complain that the Germans plan too much and that the Japanese—who like to review ideas constantly—won't make decisions. Suspicions circulate that some researchers are withholding information from the group.'

"Global homogeneity was never a desirable vision culturally, creatively, or philosophically. But now it has become clear that living with and managing diversity will be the central theme of the coming century."

In his book, Rhinesmith explores what he views as the seven key factors of multicultural team leadership:

1. Personal styles of the team members.
2. Functional cultures of team members (finance, engineering, marketing).
3. Corporate culture of the company, division, or unit represented by each team member.
4. National culture of each team member.
5. Stages of team development.
6. Effectiveness of team functioning.
7. Stage of professional development of each team member.

These management factors operate at the *team* level. Gert Hofstede's empirical research project, *Culture's Consequences* (1980), updated in *Cultures and*

Organizations (1991), overviews four major national culture variables across forty countries and examines their implications for managerial differences at the *organizational* level. Any company considering a merger or acquisition across borders involving a company from a different national culture must be conversant with this research and factor it into its cultural due diligence process.

According to Rhinesmith, most Western companies select, recruit, and reward people who are achievement-driven, control-oriented, and time-sensitive and who exhibit a *bias for action*. This is a very "American" profile, and certainly not desired in all national cultures. Other implications of national culture differences for operating a business can be seen in the area of *risk management*. People from cultures in which people feel a sense of control over their environment, typically Western cultures, will have a higher tolerance for risk than will people from cultures in which people feel constrained by their environment, typically Asian subcontinent and African cultures.

Factoring national differences in culture into the cultural due diligence process is probably best accomplished by assessing the national cultures on the same characteristics. A very useful model is presented in the book *Doing Business Internationally* (Medina-Walker, Walker, & Schmitz, 2002). The authors present and define ten characteristics of national culture that can be used for comparative analysis. These include: *environment, time, action, communications, space, power, individualism, competitiveness, structure,* and *thinking.*

Reflect on a trip you have taken out of the country and contrast your own orientation on these characteristics against that of the country visited and you will probably see the point. Did you find yourself upset by what you perceived as lack of punctuality? Being crowded on public transportation or in the marketplace? Not being able to clearly identify who was in charge? These are small but predictable examples of *culture clash* stemming from differences in national culture and, in part, the basis of the "Ugly American" stereotype. Cultures are not wrong; they just are as they are. Unfortunately, we tend to lack cultural sensitivity as individuals and organizations and expect our culture to prevail wherever we go.

A final word on the topic, again from Rhinesmith (1996): "When managing across cultures in which your company's values and behaviors are inconsistent with local culture values, it is important to fully understand local culture values, so that, when you violate them, you can do it in a culturally sensitive manner."

The Organization as a System

ASYSTEM, ACCORDING TO the current version of the Merriam-Webster dictionary, is "a regularly interacting or interdependent group of items forming a unified whole."

Organizations are systems—often quite complex systems—and a merger or acquisition involves merging or consolidating these systems into a new and effective one.

A basic system is a set of two or more elements or components that satisfies the following three conditions:

1. *The behavior of each element of a system has an effect on the behavior of the whole system.* Nothing in an organization happens in isolation. Whatever happens in one area has an impact on other areas. An obvious example is that HR departments often spend hours on is how individual staff are handled in terms of absences, vacation days, pay, grievances, and so forth. What happens or does not happen in one area impacts all other areas in terms of morale, if nothing else.

2. *The behavior of the elements of the system, and their effects on the whole system, are interdependent.* In other words, the overall organizational system has an impact on the behavior of each piece of the system, and the pieces of the

system have an impact on the whole system. In a single work unit you can see the same phenomenon in the group dynamics. The individuals have an impact on the group, and the group has an impact on each individual.

3. *However subgroups of the elements are formed, each has an effect on the behavior of the whole and none has an independent effect on it.* This means that no matter how you organize the parts of a system, you cannot isolate the system impact and it is always a two-way street; each element impacts the system and the system impacts each element no matter how you organize it.

SYSTEM AWARENESS

Rarely have we met a senior executive who disagreed with the statement that an organization is a system; however, there is often little awareness or understanding of what this means. A system-aware management group realizes that each senior manager actually has at least two hats to wear. One responsibility is to represent and champion the functions for which they are responsible, and the other is to be an advisor to the CEO on organizational system effectiveness. In this advisor role, each needs to be thinking about the operation of the total organizational system and how to best maximize overall organizational system effectiveness.

To achieve this, each senior manager must be accountable for not only his or her own area, but also for the impact the area has on the ability of every other area in the system to operate effectively. Further, when in this "advisor" role, they should also be considering and focusing on the cumulative impact of all operations for the good of the total organization. This is what it means to be *system-sensitive* and to act in a *system-aware* manner.

Understanding systems and their consequences for management is a critical skill for managing an organization at any time, but it becomes particularly critical when attempting to institute a merger or acquisition. The greater the amount of change, the more critical this system awareness becomes, especially in post-merger integration, which represents some of the most complex and comprehensive changes an organization may ever go through.

Let's take this system concept down to a relatively simple level—the performance of an individual worker in an organization—to illustrate these three system principles.

THE INDIVIDUAL AS A PERFORMANCE SYSTEM

Geary Rummler, in his very system-focused book, *Improving Performance* (1992), discusses the issue of the individual performer in the organization. He lists six areas of analysis that are critical to understanding why the individual performs or behaves the way he or she does.

The first of these is *Performance Specifications*. Do performance standards exist? And if they do exist, is the performer aware of them and does he or she have an accurate understanding of them? Also, does the performer consider these standards to be attainable?

The second area Rummler mentions is *Task Support*. Can the performer easily recognize when action is required? Can the task be done without interference from other tasks? Are the job procedures and work flow logical? Are adequate resources available for performance, such as time, tools, staff, and information?

The third area is *Consequences*. Are the consequences for performance aligned to support the desired performance? Are the consequences meaningful from the performer's viewpoint? And are consequences for performance delivered or available in a timely manner?

Rummler's fourth area is *Feedback*. Does the performer receive information about his or her performance? And if so is it relevant, accurate, timely, specific, and easy to understand?

The fifth area is *Skills and Knowledge*. The basic questions in this area are (1) Does the performer have the necessary skills and knowledge to perform? (2) Does the performer know how to perform and when? and (3) Does the performer know why the desired performance is important?

The sixth and final area Rummler proposes in the analysis of performance at the individual level is *Individual Capacity*. Is the performer physically, mentally, and emotionally able to perform?

The point is that nothing in a system operates in isolation—not even at the individual level. The worker has an impact on people and systems around him or her beyond the task or job. These in turn impact the worker. No matter how you may try to organize things, you cannot get away from this phenomenon and make the worker independent of the system, nor the system independent of the worker.

WINNING THE BATTLE WHILE LOSING THE WAR

Relationships between one area of the organizational system and another and their impact on other areas are often overlooked in a well-intentioned effort to maximize performance while treating the system's component areas in isolation.

An example: in a public utility company in which we were working, there was a recognition that the company needed to get "leaner and more business-like" to prepare for deregulation. Every department was charged with completing a comprehensive review of its own operations and "tightening up" wherever appropriate.

This resulted in the Collections Department (a part of the Finance function) engaging in a benchmarking exercise after realizing that they routinely held off on any type of collection action until an account was forty-five days in arrears. Most other companies they studied contacted customers much sooner, as early as fifteen days, with almost all triggering collections efforts by thirty days. Further, the companies that started at fifteen days had the lowest loss rate.

Given this data, the head of the Collections Unit logically decided to pursue an aggressive collections policy. He set in motion a new billing system that would generate red-bordered late notices at the fifteen-day mark. The business case indicated that the increased costs in mailing and computer services would be more than offset by the reduced writeoffs. And getting the money in sooner would also have a positive impact on funds available and cash flow.

Meanwhile, over in Customer Service, a review and benchmarking exercise had shown that they were overstaffed when compared to similar operations and, further, spent too much time, on average, on the phone with each customer.

They analyzed the calls they were getting and saw that most were simple service requests—re-lighting pilot lights or concerns about odors and possible leaks. Most of these actually resulted in scheduling a service call, and the information needed was quite simple. Additionally, however, they also received a small number of calls about bills or balances, which required more time to deal with accurately. Their benchmark data indicated considerable savings could be achieved by isolating the "account balance" calls in a small, separate unit and then instituting much tighter standards on call length for all other inquiries.

This change in their internal processes would allow them to reduce overall staffing by over 25 percent and put their staffing standards and costs more in line with what the benchmark data indicated was normal in their geographical area.

These departments' changes were implemented within thirty days of each other. As you may well imagine, the changes did not mesh together very well. When the collection notices from the Collections Department began to be received by customers, the call volume in Customer Service went up geometrically and exceeded the capability of the phone system. On some days up to 50 percent of calls were lost. Complaints of poor service to the state regulator skyrocketed, and staff in the Regulations Department had to be significantly increased—at far greater expense per head than the cost of customer service staff.

Each of these department actions, in isolation, made perfect sense, but in a system sense they were mutually destructive. In overall terms for organizational system effectiveness, they represented a minor disaster—with total costs easily exceeding the combined expected gains from both the Collections and Customer Service initiatives. We see these types of well-intended but non-systemic actions and their resultant impact on organizational effectiveness in many companies, and quite often.

Staff functions are another common source of organizational ineffectiveness through a simple lack of system awareness. In working with a computer services company in the U.K., we took on a task of improving their customer service ratings in the Service Division. This division was composed of almost two thousand people scattered across the U.K. in numerous district offices.

Customer satisfaction data was generated each year on all service suppliers in the U.K. by several industry magazines. In the year prior to our project, the client was rated as thirteenth of thirteen suppliers of service in the U.K. This obviously did not fit the company plan in a highly competitive industry that was consolidating.

The people in the division who actually saw customers were the engineers and technicians who went to the customer sites to provide routine service and resolve problems. Each of these engineers and technicians had a company vehicle, either a car or van, meaning that considerable assets were tied up in the automotive fleet.

A very conscientious accountant had done a study of fleet costs and focused on resale values. It was quite obvious that resale value of the vehicles was being negatively impacted due to poor maintenance. Potentially, significant increases in resale value could be generated by improving maintenance and upkeep across the fleet. Further, this money would fall straight to the bottom line. Standards were developed and added to the audit checklist for all field managers. However, the finance group experienced considerable trouble in getting these new standards implemented, so over time the company evolved a "successful" program that centered on a mandatory checklist for each vehicle that had to be completed at the end of each day by the district manager.

Adherence to this procedure was added to the internal audit checklist as a priority item. After all, this procedure did not take long—a few minutes per vehicle at the end of each day—and as it turned out there was already a requirement to routinely check the computer parts and equipment inventory in each vehicle, so this was combined into one daily mandatory checklist—all in all a very rational and appropriate action when considered in isolation.

Now let us return to our customer service problem. When we talked to engineers and technicians about customer service, a very clear message came through. It was abundantly clear to these people that the company and its management, in their perception, did not really care about service quality. They felt that pressure was on the staff to focus on things other than the customer and the service provided.

One of the common examples given was the need to leave the customer site in time to wash and service the vehicle and return to the office before the district manager left for the day.

An analysis of the District Office operations uncovered a major problem. The reality of life in a District Office was that any individual engineer or technician saw his or her district manager in person for roughly forty minutes per day, split relatively evenly between first thing in the morning and the end of the work day. The morning time was generally spent on giving out and reviewing the assignments and calls that needed to be completed that day. Most managers were quite good in the morning at focusing on the need for providing good service and for keeping the customers operating. But at the end of the day when the employees were coming in from a day of customer interaction, all the manager wanted to do was go over the car maintenance sheet and inventory lists with each employee.

What was the "real" message about customer service? The staff thought it was very clear: vehicle maintenance and parts inventory first, customer service a distant second. Clearly, this was not the intent of the company, nor even of the people in finance who were responsible for the regulations, but intent will always be secondary to observable behavior in terms of employee perception.

Here are some other brief examples of well-intended but non-systemic actions: cost cutting done on a department-by-department basis, with little or no system thought or sensitivity; quality initiatives limited to one or two units; productivity pushes in parts of an operation; and single department process re-engineering initiatives. Such actions, taken without system awareness or knowledge of the impact of the action on other components of the organizational system, usually detract from the effectiveness of the total organization.

CROSS-FUNCTIONAL TEAMWORK

In many companies, even the more straightforward aspects of system awareness, such as teamwork between functions or units, is usually given no thought. Covert to open warfare between units in central offices and in the field is not uncommon, in our experience. Usually this occurs in a highly competitive organizational culture, where there is no real priority given to overall organizational strategy and effectiveness. This harmful and non-systemic functional conflict occurs in spite of a simple maxim that all managers and staff could easily keep in mind: any amount of time people in an organization have to spend in dealing with each other and the organizational processes is time lost from focus on the customer, the competition, and the bottom line.

MANAGEMENT AND THE SYSTEM

One of the more grievous examples of lack of system awareness or non-systemic thinking can often be seen in senior management meetings. Each senior manager will come to the meeting well prepared to represent his or her own functional area of responsibility. Additionally, in most instances, there is an unspoken agreement that each manager will stick to his or her own area and refrain from commentary about things in peers' areas of responsibility.

This means that a senior management meeting, in which the heads of all elements of the system are in attendance, is really a series of bilateral meetings between the boss and each of the function heads. It is assumed that whatever pulling together of each of these areas into one cohesive whole is done is the responsibility of the boss, usually the CEO. Sometimes this happens—more often it does not.

What are the consequences for the senior managers? Meetings of this type model a focus on the performance of individual functions, with little or no priority on the performance of the total organizational system. This actively decreases senior management's system awareness, while reinforcing functional excellence, or the "I'm all right, Jack!" syndrome, making it entirely possible for any of the functions to be the best platoon in an army that loses the war!

SYNTHESIS BEFORE ANALYSIS

Because organizations are systems, then system theory requires that analysis must follow synthesis, not precede it. While somewhat counterintuitive, in practical terms this means that any investigation into an organizational problem should begin by first looking at all the system components surrounding the problem rather than looking within the single system component where the problem manifests itself. To solve any particular organizational problem requires first understanding and documenting how the problem unit or area in question fits into the overall system in order to determine what effect or impact the problem area is having on all other functions, units, or areas in the organizational system. Further, the impact that these other areas have on the problem area must also be determined.

For example, what impact does the introduction of a new inventory management system by the Distribution Department have on the Training Department, on Customer Service, on Finance, and so forth, and what factors in those areas impact the introduction of the system in Distribution?

Going further, it means that making any type of change to any part of the system requires the same type of investigation—again, synthesis must precede analysis. The change must be checked to ascertain whether it is a positive change for the rest of the system and whether the rest of the system can support it, rather than simply making a well-intended unilateral change and disrupting the larger system.

To further illustrate the point of system interdependence, here is an analogy we heard once from one of the world's better systems thinkers, Russell Ackoff. He said that if you wanted to build a custom car and went out and bought the absolutely best carburetor on the market, the best distributor, the best transmission, the best suspension, the best axles, the best wheels, and so on—you would end up assembling a car that would not run. Each part would have been optimized in isolation, but the combination would not work. A system needs a set of parts that not only perform their own functions well, but that perform these functions in concert with all the other system components.

All managers in the organization must become as concerned and aware of the impact of their parts of the organization on the effectiveness of the rest of the organizational system as they are of the operations of their own areas. The higher the manager's position in the organization, the more critical this knowledge and system awareness become to the organization as a whole.

CULTURE IS NOT A SYSTEM COMPONENT

We have already discussed the definition of organizational culture. Taking the simpler definition of organizational culture as "the way we do things around here," let's look a little deeper at this concept.

The drivers of "the way we do things around here" are multiple. In fact, culture, even more than many other characteristics of the organization, is deeply embedded in the overall system and also a product of the system. Returning briefly to some examples of organizational system issues that were discussed previously, the connections to the organization's culture underline how systemic and pervasive the culture actually is in an organization.

At the computer services company with the customer service problems, we discussed the issue of district managers talking about customers in the morning when assignments were made, but never mentioning them in the evening when the engineer or technician returned to the office after dealing with customers all day, focusing instead on vehicle maintenance and inventory. Obviously, this situation had a negative impact on the levels of customer service provided by the engineers and technicians, who were receiving a mixed message about the priority of customer service. It is a clear example of a way that "how we do things around here" can be erroneously derived from procedural requirements and observation of one manager's behavior.

At the public utility company (where actions in the Collections Department impacted what was happening in the Customer Service Department), the general reaction toward the mutually negative impact of actions taken in isolation was wry amusement on the part of management and the feeling that each department had done its part. This company clearly had a functionally driven culture, which emanated from executive and senior management. There was no overall focus on what was good for the company, and the customers were more of an afterthought. There was also the older utility mindset that the customers had no choice of providers anyway, so why worry about it. These two factors had a direct and strongly negative bearing on "how we do things here."

Daily behavior of management is a major driver of culture. People focus on what managers do—on observable behavior—rather than on what they say. Messages about "the way we do things" are inferred from all aspects of management behavior or, in the words of one anonymous staff member, "What you do speaks so loudly that I cannot hear what you say!"

The key point here is that culture is deeply embedded within the organizational system. It cannot be taken out and dealt with in isolation. Culture is not amenable to being treated independently and attempts to do so will almost invariably result in failure.

An article in *Psychology Today* (Reynolds, 1987) is a detailed account of an attempt to alter the internal culture of a company and how it probably resulted in speeding up the company's demise, rather than helping it become more effective. In this particular example, the criticality of management behavior is also made very clear.

The primary mistake the company made was trying to deal with culture as an isolated part of the organization, rather than treating culture as a manifestation of the system and dealing with it in a systemic and systematic manner. The company also seemed to think that daily management behavior, particularly at the upper levels, was somehow invisible and separate from the overall organizational culture and did not have to be aligned with it. One of the more glaring missteps taken was the manner in which the "official" culture was developed.

One of the key principles and purposes for the culture initiative that was stated early on as a primary reason for the activity was the desire to "preserve the free and open atmosphere of a 'start up' company even after the organization became a big company." The company then proceeded to develop the corporate culture document in a series of secret meetings, strictly following the chain of command. The most senior executives would develop the initial draft without any consultation; middle managers were then asked to approve and endorse this document in meetings under the guise of "discussing the document." In this case, the manner of developing the culture document was in direct contradiction to the values the document espoused.

Consequently, the culture document was not taken seriously when it was announced to the organization. With no thorough analysis of the reality of the organizational system, the espoused culture document was totally out of step with daily work life in the company. Couple this with no reasoned acknowledgment of this reality from management, and no announced plan as to how to bring reality into step with the "desired" behaviors, and the document only served to highlight how out of touch senior management was with the organizational system. The net result of this organizational culture initiative was an erosion of trust and faith in management and of the potential success of the company.

For culture change efforts to be successful, we must help organizational leaders remember that their culture is a result of and not a component of the overall organizational system and that the system includes many subcultures derived from organizational history, operational function, national culture, level of autonomy, and so on.

Organizational System Alignment

O RGANIZATIONAL ALIGNMENT IS A PROCESS that seeks to improve the effectiveness of the organizational system based on results of a diagnosis of the organization's current situation, intended direction, and desired results. This diagnosis should be both *systemic* and *systematic* in nature and examine the organization as a total system of dynamic interactive components. (See Figure 3.1.)

We base our initial diagnosis on a modification of the Organizational Alignment Model (Tosti & Jackson, 1987) and conduct our detailed organizational system diagnosis through what we call the *Organizational Scan* process. The results are of tremendous value for determining the best and most effective actions to take to resolve issues confronting the organization, sequencing them, and putting them into effect.

In other words, the nature of the problem or challenge dictates the design and sequence of the *optimum* solutions that are applied across the organizational system. This data-based method is far different and, in our experience, a superior approach to the typical solution-based approaches that use training, process re-engineering, Balanced Scorecard, and other popular methods to "fix" the organization. These tend to be based on an insufficient diagnosis and result in a high-stakes trial-and-error play.

We have designed and proven the Organizational Scan process to be efficient, comprehensive, and thorough, and we typically use it over a few weeks rather than months. The rich and detailed information obtained more than justifies the time that the Organizational Scan requires and provides a sound basis for all subsequent actions and initiatives required to increase the organization's current and future effectiveness and success.

A SYSTEMIC APPROACH

All organizations are systems in which many factors have a bearing on why people behave the way they do in any given situation on any given day. A fundamental key to effective change is to first ascertain what factors, both formal and informal, are driving the current system. Second is to plan for altering or modifying those factors needed to support and sustain the new desired performance.

Figure 3.1. Organizational Alignment Model

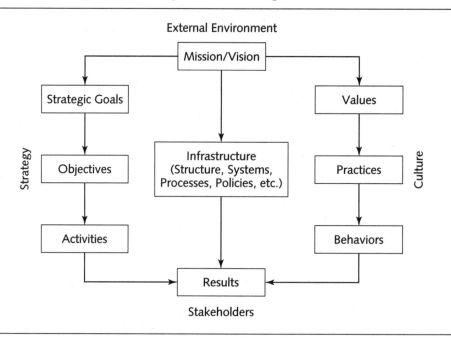

Source: Based on Tosti & Jackson, 1987.

Our own Organizational Alignment Model, shown in Figure 3.1, is a solid, proven, and highly intuitive diagnostic template for initial diagnosis of the organizational system drivers. (Appendix B presents a fuller description of the model, definitions of terms, and examples that can be used to help clients understand the concepts as they embark on the process. This is also included on the CD-ROM that is included with the book.)

GETTING THE BALANCE RIGHT

The Organizational Alignment Model shows the organization in the context of an increasingly turbulent *External Environment* and then guides analysis of three interdependent drivers of organizational *results*:

- Strategy
- Culture
- Infrastructure

It also shows the organization's *Stakeholders* as the evaluators of *Organizational Result*. The *Stakeholder* community includes those with a vested interest in the organization's success, for example, a parent company, customers, investors, shareholders, staff and management, suppliers, the local community, and so on.

AN ORGANIZATIONAL SYSTEM MODEL

If managers are going to look at the organization as a system as a matter of routine, as we advised in the last chapter, a model is needed to help them sort out the complexity and guide them as to what to look for and where to look. Some manner of keeping track of where you are and where you have been in the analysis of problems and opportunities is sorely needed.

In an attempt to fill this need, in 1979 Bob Carleton and Donald Tosti developed the Organizational System Model, shown in Figure 3.2. Since an organization is essentially a group of people working together to achieve valued results, the idea was to incorporate both the industrial engineering model of work and the sociological model of work. In the classic engineering model of work, a set of conditions exists within which a process operates to deliver an output. The sociological

Figure 3.2. Organizational System Model: Organizational Focus

	CONDITIONS	PROCESS	OUTPUTS
ORGANIZATION	**Direction** • Business situation • Mission/vision • Strategy • Structure • Goals	**Systems** • Planning • Policy/procedure • Support • Information systems • Budgeting • Monitoring	**Results** • Success measures • Profitability • Competitive position • Stakeholder satisfaction
PEOPLE	**Culture** • Ideal values • Actual values • Climate • Objectives and demands • Expectations • Politics	**Leadership/Management** • Practices/behaviors • Selection/development • Reward/recognition • Skill/knowledge • Motivation/feedback	**Productivity** • Performance levels • Morale • Empowerment • Loyalty/commitment • Business awareness • Continuous improvement
WORK	**Resources** • Workload • Schedules/cycles • Tools/equipment • Data/information • Physical environment	**Methods** • Work processes • Resource allocation • Process monitoring • In-process correction • SOPs	**Products/Services** • Product/service delivery • Customer satisfaction • Quality • Quantity • Service levels

Source: From Carleton & Tosti (1979).

model has work being performed by people within an organization. These two models, while theoretically simple, do seem to account for the critical elements that need to be understood in order to analyze the performance of an organizational system.

Since that time we have added a number of adjustments to the model that experience, research, and advancements in the understanding of organizations have shown to be useful. The first of these was the development of another row, focused on *external factors* of the organizational system. Figure 3.3 presents these external factors.

Figure 3.3. Addition to the Organizational System Model: External Focus

	CONDITIONS	PROCESS	OUTPUTS
EXTERNAL FACTORS	**Marketplace** • World economy • Geopolitical climate • Regulation • Competitors • Technology • Location • Business cycle	**Investment** • Strategic alliances • Partnerships • Mergers and acquisitions • New product development • Privatization • IPOs	**Positioning** • Market share/ dominance • Economies of scale/scope • Reduced vulnerability • Increased revenue • Globalization • New markets

This new row represents the areas of the organization's perception of and direct response to the external environment in which it operates.

The second major adjustment we have made to the original model is to clarify what is and is not in the *People/Conditions* box, which we have now labeled *Values and Beliefs* rather than Culture. As we began to work with and understand the nature of organizational culture, we came to realize that labeling this particular box as "culture" would lead people to think or believe something that is simply not true. *Culture, in a system sense, does not exist in, nor even primarily reside in, one particular box of the system.* Organizational culture, and the components of the organizational system that drive and maintain it, are distributed *throughout* the system. Organizational culture and its drivers are far more systemic in nature than are most other aspects of the organization.

It is important to note that, for any given situation, there may well be a number of elements that, although listed in one of the boxes, will have little or no practical bearing on that situation. Our intent in developing the model was to assure that no potentially relevant data were overlooked, so we included everything that COULD have a bearing. This model forms a checklist of sorts so that a particular area for inquiry must be consciously excluded, rather than inadvertently overlooked.

The Organizational System Scan Model, which reflects our *current* understanding of the dynamics of an organizational system, is presented in Figure 3.4.

Figure 3.4. Organizational System Scan Model

	CONDITIONS	PROCESS	OUTPUTS
EXTERNAL FACTORS	**Marketplace** • World economy • Geopolitical climate • Regulation • Competitors • Technology • Location • Business cycle	**Investment** • Strategic alliances • Partnerships • Mergers and acquisitions • New product development • Privatization • IPOs	**Positioning** • Market share/dominance • Economies of scale/scope • Reduced vulnerability • Increased revenue • Globalization • New markets
ORGANIZATION	**Direction** • Business situation • Mission/vision • Strategy • Structure • Goals	**Systems** • Planning • Policy/procedure • Support • Information systems • Budgeting • Monitoring	**Results** • Success measures • Profitability • Competitive position • Stakeholder satisfaction
PEOPLE	**Values and Beliefs** • Ideal values • Actual values • Climate • Objectives and demands • Expectations • Politics	**Leadership/Management** • Practices/behaviors • Selection/development • Reward/recognition • Skill/knowledge • Motivation/feedback	**Productivity** • Performance levels • Morale • Empowerment • Loyalty/commitment • Business awareness • Continuous improvement
WORK	**Resources** • Workload • Schedules/cycles • Tools/equipment • Data/information • Physical environment	**Methods** • Work processes • Resource allocation • Process monitoring • In-process correction • SOPs	**Products/Services** • Product/service delivery • Customer satisfaction • Quality • Quantity • Service levels

This model can be used to guide systemic and systematic collection of data on the current "Is" and desired "Should" organizational situations, as perceived by employees in various functions. Using the model assures that no component of the system will be overlooked.

In each box of the model we have listed elements within the organizational system that should be included in that particular category. These lists are not intended to be all-inclusive, but only to serve as examples.

Let's start a brief review of the model's elements with the top row of Figure 3.4, External Factors.

The first box on the left, Marketplace, is intended to cover the Conditions that the External Factors place on the organization. Any and all of the listed elements can have a direct bearing on the strategic direction of the organization in response to marketplace characteristics, for example, the world economy, the business cycle, or actions of competitors, among many possibilities.

The box under Process, labeled Investment, represents the organization's response to the Marketplace conditions (External Factors) that were identified in the first box. The Investment area includes things like formation of strategic alliances and partnerships, embarking on a strategy of mergers and acquisitions, the formation of alliances, instituting new product development, or, in some instances, moving from a public agency to a private company or going public with an IPO.

This leads to the organizational Outputs box, or the results of the Investment that was made. This checklist is to help the organization raise appropriate questions about market share or dominance, economies of scale, vulnerability to external factors, increased revenue through better response to external factors, moves to broaden the market by going global, and entering new product markets.

The items in each of these boxes, although representing distinct areas of inquiry, do not exist in a vacuum and all interact with one another. In other words, the elements in any particular box of the model have a potential impact on the system characteristics residing in any other box.

Let's look at the boxes of the model that are focused within the organization rather than external factors. These are broken out in Figures 3.5, 3.6, and 3.7. Let's look at the Work Level first.

Starting with the organization's work, the bottom row of the complete model shown in Figure 3.4, the work Conditions are labeled as Resources, meaning what

Figure 3.5. Organizational Factors: Work Level

	CONDITIONS	PROCESS	OUTPUTS
	Resources	**Methods**	**Products/Services**
WORK	• Workload	• Work processes	• Product/service delivery
	• Schedules/cycles	• Resource allocation	• Customer satisfaction
	• Tools/equipment	• Process monitoring	• Quality
	• Data/information	• In-process correction	• Quantity
	• Physical environment	• SOPs	• Service levels

is available for use in performing the work. In this category we include the tools and equipment used in performing the work, the schedules and work cycles that are involved in doing the work, the data and information about the work that is available to workers, and the physical environment within which the work is performed.

Utilizing these Resources, the work Process then occurs by means of various Methods to actually do the work. Methods includes the physical processes that people use, the resources allocated to accomplish any part of the work, monitoring of the process of doing the work, and the in-process correction information and methods that are part of doing the work, as well as any standard operating procedures (SOPs) that may exist for how the work should be done.

The process of doing the work produces Products and Services, which are the main organizational Outputs. The Products and Services delivered are the main reason for the organization's existence and, as such, they are worthy of a bit more analysis, although product/service delivery is indeed the starting point in this box. Going further, one must ask what is the customer satisfaction with Products or Services; what is the quality and quantity of the products and services delivered; and what is the perceived service level.

We can see that just the WORK being performed by the organization is in and of itself a reasonably complex system, requiring considerable coordination and interdependency to meet the needs of customers. Breakdowns or deficiencies in any of the items listed in the boxes can have consequences for the organization as a whole and for the viability of the product or service. All of this system complexity is in existence prior to our considering the fact that the work is being performed

Figure 3.6. Organizational Factors: People Level

	CONDITIONS	PROCESS	OUTPUTS
	Values and Beliefs	**Leadership/Management**	**Productivity**
PEOPLE	• Ideal values • Actual values • Climate • Objectives and demands • Expectations • Politics	• Practices/behaviors • Selection/development • Reward/recognition • Skill/knowledge • Motivation/feedback	• Performance levels • Morale • Empowerment • Loyalty/commitment • Business awareness • Continuous improvement

by People, which is the next row as we move up the Organizational System Scan Model. The addition of people to the mix, of course, brings it's own rich complexity. See Figure 3.6.

In the People row, we start with the Values and Beliefs that the workforce bring with them, as well as those that are fundamental to the organization's culture. These include elements like the ideal values or espoused values to which the organization aspires. These ideal values do not always match the actual values or "real" values that are held by the organization's people. The overall climate within which the people perform is another basic People condition, as are the work objectives or work demands placed on people, the expectations the people have of themselves and each other, and the inevitable politics, or use of power and privilege, that seems to be a universal component of People endeavors, desired or not.

This rich mix of People conditions is then applied to actually performing the work, which is done under the auspices of Leadership and Management, used here to represent the function of leading and managing people, not titles or boxes on the organizational chart. It is not unusual for a highly respected colleague to functionally provide more leadership in a particular situation than does the designated supervisor for any particular group of workers.

Included in this category are elements like the practices and behaviors of the Leadership and Management function that drive the practices and behaviors of those performing the work on a daily basis, how job selection is made, who performs what, and how people are developed for advancement, as well as formal and informal reward and recognition systems. Also included are the actual skills and knowledge of the people and how they are developed and maintained, the motivation of the people doing the work, and the nature and manner of feedback that is provided.

The elements of Values and Beliefs that make up the basic People Conditions, together with the Leadership and Management of the Work Process, all have a bearing on the Output that the people produce, or their Productivity.

Productivity, the output of the People level of the organizational system, begins with the measurement or quantification of the performance levels being achieved. There are many other components of overall Productivity, including elements like the general morale of the people that results from the organization's work processes and its leadership and management, how empowered they are in making decisions and taking action in the performance of the work, the degree of loyalty and commitment to the work and the organization, and the general level of business awareness on the part of the people, as well as any continuous improvement processes applied to the Outputs of the organization. All have a direct bearing on overall organizational Productivity.

We have now covered a representative list of the system variables that impact on overall organizational effectiveness in terms of *the work itself and the people doing the work*. We now have to add the factors that the Organization itself brings to this system complexity, shown in Figure 3.7.

The conditions that the Organization level brings to the performance of work are generally the overall Direction that the organization is trying to take in the marketplace by means of its people and processes. This includes things like the current business situation, the mission and vision of the organization and how clear

Figure 3.7.   Organizational Factors: Organization Level

	CONDITIONS	PROCESS	OUTPUTS
ORGANIZATION	**Direction** • Business situation • Mission/vision • Strategy • Structure • Goals	**Systems** • Planning • Policy/procedure • Support • Information systems • Budgeting • Monitoring	**Results** • Success measures • Profitability • Competitive position • Stakeholder satisfaction

and well understood they are at all levels of the organization, the business strategy, the structure the organization has chosen to implement the strategy, and the broad goals of the organization. These organizational Direction elements occur repeatedly at multiple levels in the organization—unit, department, division, or however the organizational structure is broken down—and any analysis must incorporate an assessment of how well-aligned these directional elements of the system are from level to level in the organization.

These organizational conditions then translate into the broad governing processes of an organization or its Systems for guiding and controlling the work Process. This box includes things like planning, the development and dissemination of policies and procedures, organizational support provided to the work process, the information systems, budgeting, and monitoring the work effort.

Hopefully, all this organizational systems process applied to the people in the performance of the work will deliver valuable organizational Outputs, which we label simply as Results. Even here, however, it is not a matter of a simple measure. A number of variables must be considered to fully understand the organizational results. Besides basic success measures, there are issues of overall profitability, the resulting competitive position, and most importantly, stakeholder satisfaction. It is important to note that the "stakeholders" include not only shareholders but also staff, customers, suppliers, and the community within which the organization operates.

These nine boxes of the Organizational System Scan Model, covering the external as well as internal aspects of the organizational system, clearly are a very complex mix of system variables, all of which must be considered in creating and maintaining an effective and efficient new organization. The value of the model is as a comprehensive, systemic template to use when considering the organizational system as a whole. It also helps to assure that no relevant system variable is left out when analyzing organizational problems and opportunities or when designing and implementing changes.

Most of the problems that organizational managers and executives deal with are not, in actuality, as simple and contained as they may assume at first blush. In fact, many of the common deficiencies encountered in organizations today are, in effect, self-inflicted by the management of the organization when they take actions that do not take into account the systemic nature of the organization. A simple or obvious solution developed in one function of the organization can have an impact on a number of other areas, and total organizational effectiveness can be diminished far beyond any potential gain in the particular function, as the examples in earlier chapters showed.

Also, many experienced managers are familiar with what we term "Lazarus Problems," problems that apparently rise from the dead. No matter how many times a problem has been resolved and buried, it just keeps coming back. This phenomenon is usually the result of the rest of the system reacting to an initial solution to a problem and forcing things back to the way they were. As we said earlier, solutions implemented without consideration of the entire organizational system often suppress (for a while) but do not really solve problems.

Changes to a system, if they are to have any hope for long-term success, require systemic changes implemented in a systematic manner. Changes made and maintained in this manner will last and create a new reality in the organization. (Appendix C presents a brief overview of the Organizational Scan Model, which is also included on the CD-ROM accompanying this book.)

CHECKING THE VITAL SIGNS

A periodic organizational scan is as necessary to maintain the health and viability of an organization as is a thorough periodic physical exam to the maintenance of the physical health of a person. Like a thorough physical, an organizational scan can be a critical element in prescribing preventive medicine.

Periodic scans, done systematically and in a system-aware manner, will help the forward-thinking executive responsible for the effectiveness of the organization to avoid problems and access opportunities far more effectively and efficiently.

In Exhibit 3.1 we present the purpose for and list a number of valuable benefits of an organizational scan. Additionally, for those who wish to explore the utility and nature of this model more thoroughly, in Appendix D we have provided a partial list of sample probes that could be used when undergoing a thorough examination of Conditions under External Factors: Marketplace and Organizational Direction, each of the boxes in the model.

It should be quite clear after our discussion in the past three chapters that the achievement of post-merger success, that is, efficiently implementing an integrated business plan supported by an aligned and integrated culture, requires a systemic analysis of all potentially relevant variables.

Very little in organizational life has as much likelihood of making a broad impact and producing great change in daily operations as does the merger of two

---

Exhibit 3.1.   Overview of the Organizational System Scan Model

---

Purpose   To gather current data on the *"organizational situation,"* as perceived by its functions and people, for use in decision making by top management. The *Organizational Scan* clarifies organizational intent and direction and captures information about the "real organization's" alignment with its values and belief system, day-to-day life, and priorities—in short, its culture. It also assesses relevance and helpfulness of organizational systems, policies, and procedures.

Benefits

- Provides the CEO/top management with an efficient and comprehensive diagnostic scan of the organization at all levels;
- Identifies potential areas of greatest leverage for increasing organizational effectiveness as desired;
- Indicates priorities for action to move/transform the organization, which serves to focus and facilitate planning;
- Provides an assessment of the organization's readiness for change and of the adequacy of the organization's leadership and management to effect that change; and, perhaps most significantly,
- Enables the alignment of the organization's strategy, culture, and infrastructure to the business reality confronting it.

---

organizations. Therefore a model like the Organizational Systems Scan Model can be extremely valuable to executive and consultant alike. The issues are many and complex, and the model can be invaluable in helping an organization sort out and organize all of the data.

Further, this model helps to bring out the organizational culture issues that are woven into the fabric of the organizational system.

Dealing with organizational culture can be a very perilous activity indeed. While such an effort has the potential to improve organizational results dramatically, it also has the ability to measurably diminish them. Culture initiatives in general will either make things work considerably better, or make them considerably worse. It is never neutral in impact.

In the next section we discuss our method for cultural due diligence and assessment, a method with the potential to considerably lessen the negative impact of cultural changes during mergers and acquisitions.

Cultural Due Diligence and Assessment

Part 2 of this book consists of two chapters:

- Chapter 4: Overview of Cultural Due Diligence
- Chapter 5: Performing Cultural Due Diligence

Chapter 4 provides an overview of the Cultural Due Diligence (CDD) process that we recommend. In this chapter we discuss traditional due diligence, make a case for inclusion of CDD, discuss off-the-shelf versus customized cultural assessment tools, present our customized CDD model and its deliverables, and discuss due diligence and legal restrictions and retention of key personnel.

In Chapter 5 we discuss the importance of both quantitative and qualitative data in the CDD process and walk through the twelve domains of our CDD model, providing examples of each domain.

Figure I.2 provides an outline of the due diligence activities we recommend and follow in our own practice.

Figure I.2. Cultural Due Diligence and Assessment

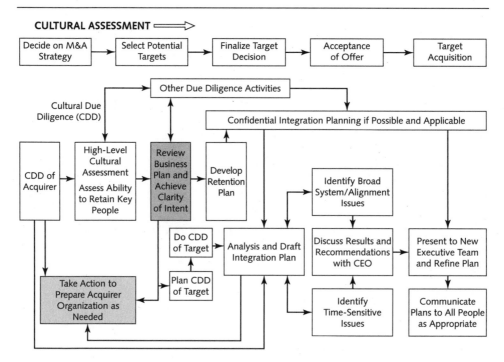

Overview of Cultural Due Diligence

D UE DILIGENCE, MOST SIMPLY, is the investigation of one party by another party to gather information that will assist in decision making and risk analyses. It is done in conjunction with transactions between people or companies—ranging from buying a home at one end of the continuum to multi-billion-dollar corporate mergers and acquisitions at the other. Definitions vary, but common to all is the purchaser attempting to find any skeletons in the closet that may sour the deal. It is a formalized and detailed outgrowth of the centuries-old concept of caveat emptor—let the buyer beware. In mergers and acquisitions, due diligence has come to mean "a series of exploratory activities used in evaluation of a target company prior to finalization of the merger or acquisition" (Clemente & Greenspan, 1998). Traditional due diligence focuses primarily on the financial, legal, regulatory, and tax issues through the processes of disclosure and discovery.

Exhibit 4.1 shows the categories and areas of examination of a traditional comprehensive due diligence.

Exhibit 4.1. Traditional Due Diligence Checklist

General Corporate Information
- Corporate history
- Company organization and equity structure
- Corporate structure
- Corporate formation documents

Management
- Management profiles and contracts
- Management reporting and controls
- Management compensation and other agreements

Industry, Market, and Competitor Assessment
- Industry overview
- Market overview
- Competitive situation
- Company positioning and exit strategies

Financial Information
- Financial statements with supporting information
- Budgets and projections
- Internal controls
- Indebtedness

Assets and Facilities
- Capital assets
- Current assets

Intellectual Property

Contingent Liabilities

Tax Information
- Tax return documentation
- Tax audit information

Legal Information
- Litigation and claims summary
- Past and present employee claims
- Other issues of legal compliance
- Other legal correspondence

Exhibit 4.1. (Continued)

Insurance

Sales and Marketing
- Products and services overview
- Pricing and profitability model
- Product development strategy
- Sales overview
- Marketing overview

Customers
- Current customer review
- Sales prospects and pipeline validation
- Channel and distributor relationship assessment

Strategic Alliances
- Distribution channels
- Strategic vendors
- Licensing and franchising agreements

CULTURAL DUE DILIGENCE

However, even in the face of a dismal M&A track record, a decade of indisputable evidence documenting that culture clash problems are the cause of most M&A failure or poor performance, and a known body of knowledge on organizational culture, the due diligence process rarely, if ever, takes into consideration the dynamics of the two organizations' cultures, their degree of compatibility, or the potential culture clashes that are almost sure to arise after the deal is done. Because of this, we believe that *cultural due diligence* can and should be a part of the due diligence process in any merger or acquisition.

In the simplest terms, Cultural Due Diligence (CDD) is a diagnostic process conducted to ascertain the degree of cultural alignment or compatibility between companies that are party to a merger or acquisition. It provides data at a sufficient level of detail to determine potential areas of culture clash and the level of difficulty these areas represent, and it is used to develop an effective integration/alignment plan to deal with the impact of organizational culture on the merger or acquisition. CDD should be viewed as a *mandatory* step to maximize post-merger or acquisition organizational effectiveness and profitability.

THE CASE FOR CULTURAL DUE DILIGENCE

Cultural Due Diligence (CDD) is a systemic, systematic, and research-based methodology for significantly increasing the odds of success of mergers, acquisitions, and alliances. It is an until-recently overlooked parallel process to the traditional financial and legal due diligence that is considered absolutely essential to any merger or acquisition.

As stated earlier, the research data on why some 55 to 77 percent of mergers and acquisitions fail in meeting their intended results is absolutely clear: the failures are overwhelmingly attributable to "culture clash" that occurs as attempts to bring the two organizations together are made, which makes merging the two organizational cultures or establishing a new culture for the merged organization extremely difficult, if not impossible.

In those instances where the organizations are merged, the ongoing direct and indirect costs of unresolved "culture clash" issues are high, and requires the merged organization to focus on internal issues and problems rather than on the marketplace, the customers, and the competition.

The CDD process is proactive problem solving in advance. By assessing the characteristics of both organizations' cultures as soon as possible in the merger process potential culture clash problems can be predicted, prioritized, and focused on and a comprehensive Cultural Integration Plan can be developed to build a new culture that takes into account all the issues and potential landmines that are a part of the terrain.

Cultural Due Diligence is as vital and necessary as are traditional legal and financial due diligence in providing an informed basis for executive decision making, risk analysis, and planning—and perhaps even more important than traditional due diligence for increasing the odds of success of the merger or acquisition.

Cultural Due Diligence is a sign of sound leadership and management. It offers decision makers in both organizations a comprehensive, data-based way to predict culture clash problems that may occur, to assess the relative importance of those problems, and to make recommendations on how to eliminate the causes or minimize the impact.

Cultural Due Diligence is appropriate in a number of key business situations, including:

- When considering mergers and acquisitions as a growth strategy;
- When selecting target companies for merger or acquisition;

- When finalizing a decision to do the deal or not;

- Immediately after execution of a letter of acceptance by the target company;

- Immediately after finalization and approval of the merger or acquisition; and/or

- As "cultural triage" after the merger or acquisition becomes effective, to deal with culture clash problems that surface.

The research cited in the three previous chapters is absolutely clear and unequivocal: Cultural Due Diligence can be overlooked only at the risk of the success of the merger or acquisition.

Performing full Cultural Due Diligence requires the following major steps in the sequence indicated.

1. Acquirer Self-Assessment

"Know thyself" is sound advice in this case. Most companies do not have detailed assessments of their own cultures, but rather live in them and make assumptions about them. A current assessment of the acquiring company's culture is essential for comparison with those of target companies to indicate degree of difficulty of cultural integration and potential culture clash problems.

2. Assessment of Potential Target Companies

If several target companies are under consideration, high-level Cultural Due Diligence can help ascertain the degree of cultural compatibility and respective cultural fit of each.

3. Detailed Cultural Assessment of Target Company

A full and detailed cultural assessment of the selected target company and comparison with that of the acquiring company is essential for building the Cultural Integration Plan.

4. Alignment/Integration Planning

Informed, data-based design of the overall Cultural Integration Plan and specification of integration/alignment initiatives, implementation sequence, and evaluation measures.

OFF-THE-SHELF VS. CUSTOMIZED CULTURAL ASSESSMENTS

Organizations that wish to assess and profile their culture, and perhaps the culture of a target company, in conjunction with Cultural Due Diligence are faced with a choice between "off-the-shelf" assessment models and "customized" assessment models. While there has been significant advancement in the understanding of organizational culture over the last ten years, the overall field is still in its infancy. At this time there is no single unified theory or assessment model of organizational culture that can anticipate and account for all the potential variables of any given organizational culture.

There are currently at least twenty-five off-the-shelf attributional models of organizational culture in existence—all based on quantitative measurement of assumed cultural factors or attributes. The developers of these models have been able to demonstrate statistically that the variables (attributes), or at least some of the variables that they profess to measure, can be measured reliably.

These attributional models provide no color or granularity of local cultural variations and so require subsequent qualitative research for effective cultural integration. Further, they introduce the confusion of a new non-business vocabulary coined to describe certain behaviors to the organization. They are predicated on the assumption that one size fits all. It does not.

Each model contains some of the assumed cultural variables, but there is no reliable commonality among these various instruments. Each model was developed from intense study of a few companies, but to arbitrarily choose any one of them for use in any given company is to commit a classic type II research error—to assume that the attributes of one group apply to a different group when it has already been established that these are different groups representing different variables—to fail to reject a null hypothesis when it is false.

Another issue is that the current attributional models measure at a very high level of abstraction. Even if a model with the right variables is chosen for the company in question, it is still necessary to interpret how the variables relate to daily work behaviors. The only way to get accurate data is to engage in qualitative data—detailed interviews, focus groups, and observations.

Also, none of the current models distinguishes between value-based differences and non-value-based differences. A brief example of the problem: two companies are merging. One has a culture that involves extensive use of e-mail and the other does not use e-mail. In this instance it is simply an issue of availability of technology, and there is no inherent value system underlying the difference. In this case the integration of the two cultures around this difference could well be limited to providing e-mail technology and a simple training program.

But now consider two other companies with the same difference in e-mail usage who are about to merge. One company has made a conscious value-based decision to severely limit e-mail usage, as it is believed that professionals should talk directly rather than send e-mails to a person down the corridor, as this is considered to be impersonal and rude.

The other company has made a conscious value-based decision to utilize e-mail almost exclusively, as it is felt that true professionals do not interrupt one another by simply dropping by another's office. Thus, courtesy requires sending an e-mail that the recipient can access when desired, as dropping in is perceived to be rude and non-professional. Now you have a value-based difference and a potential culture clash. The merging of these two cultures is not simply a matter of providing e-mail technology and training. Indeed, this probably would exacerbate the problem rather than resolve it.

This would require careful integration planning and change management, with particular attention paid to values, feelings, emotions, and pre-conceived ideas. We know no attributional model that will uncover this distinction. Distinguishing between value-based and non-value-based differences requires in-depth qualitative research consisting of interviews, focus groups, and observation to ascertain the nature and depth of the values and feelings—and often requires intensive, focused, and customized quantitative research as well.

Then there is the issue of *granularity*—breadth and depth of the cultural assessment. Is it detailed enough to distinguish between units and divisions and geography in the organizational cultures being studied? This level of granularity is critical to a responsive and prescriptive integration plan. Different parts of any given company will have subtle and not so subtle differences in their alignment with the overall organization's culture. Producing an effective integration plan for each area of the company requires some level of interviews and/or focus groups and/or targeted surveys designed to measure the particular variables at play in each area.

In summary, cultural assessment instruments and surveys that are currently available and that are based on attributional models falsely assume that a limited and pre-determined set of variables account for all cultural differences; do not provide sufficient local color to make the necessary connections between the measured attributes and daily behavior clear and understandable; do not attempt to measure all the many unique variables of an organization's culture that may be in play; provide no distinctions between value-based differences and non-value based-differences; and do not provide sufficient local granularity to allow for informed calibration for local unit or division uniqueness. Therefore, additional qualitative research is almost always required.

A simpler and more efficient approach, then, is to use a *customized culture assessment model* initially, utilizing a qualitative research design based on a *functional model* of culture. Such a functional model does not pretend to describe or assume all of the cultural attributes of the organization. Instead, it defines the areas of daily organizational life in which cultural differences play out and gathers in-depth qualitative data to, in one process, ascertain the variables that exist and determine how they play out in daily behavior.

Using such a functional model also enables the cultural researcher to subsequently design a focused and customized quantitative survey if desired. This survey, usually web based, can be sent out to both organizations' populations to gather further information on the depth and breadth of the now identified critical variables by function, department, area, and geographic location. This information provides the detail necessary to develop and implement a customized and informed integration plan specific to the two companies involved in the merger or acquisition.

An example: recently a client was considering the use of an off-the-shelf qualitative culture survey. This particular survey measures twelve assumed cultural attributes with 120 survey items. It also provides up to an additional thirty-nine supplemental survey items for selection by the client. No qualitative data is collected or reported.

In our opinion, it was highly doubtful that something this generic was going to provide the detail necessary to uncover the subtleties and nuances of culturally driven differences in daily behavior across a global organization of over 100,000 employees in more than twenty countries, with at least four separate and distinct company subcultures—all alive and well. The client agreed.

An in-depth qualitative research design, however, does not have these limitations. A well-designed series of interviews and focus groups and observations coupled with a customized and focused quantitative survey unique to the organization will yield a wealth of qualitative and quantitative data that is rich and robust, and of great utility and value.

CHARACTERISTICS OF A CUSTOMIZED CDD MODEL

As any sound organizational research should, the CDD process we have developed employs both qualitative and quantitative data collection and includes interviews, focus groups, workplace observations, documentation reviews, and customized web-based CDD surveys.

Our normal approach to analyzing and organizing CDD data is to group the findings within the twelve domains of the CDD process shown below (Carleton, 1997), although the data also can be organized around the key elements of the business plan or in any other manner that will be of greatest value to the two organizations.

CDD Cultural Domains

1. Intended direction and results

2. Key measures

3. Key business drivers

4. Infrastructure

5. Organizational practices

6. Leadership/management practices

7. Supervisory practices

8. Work practices

9. Technology use

10. Physical environment

11. Perceptions and expectations

12. Cultural indicators and artifacts

The data analysis will detail specific findings as relevant by function, company, geographic area, and any other necessary groupings to make the data most helpful to the organizations.

CDD DELIVERABLES

All of the data collected by means of the CDD process must be carefully analyzed and organized into a number of extremely valuable management tools to be used by executives and senior management in planning the integration of the two organizational cultures into a desired new culture for the merged organization. These tools include:

- Detailed cultural profiles of both organizations;
- Baseline perceptions from various constituencies of both organizations about current culture and the merger or acquisition;
- Specification of cultural similarities within the twelve cultural domains;
- Specification of cultural differences within the twelve cultural domains;
- Prediction, specification, and prioritization of "culture clash" problems and their impact on the merger;
- Estimation of degree of difficulty in integrating the two cultures;
- Specific recommendations on ways to avoid and/or minimize culture clash problems during integration; and
- Integration road map for implementation of recommendations.

Given this information and these management tools, key decisions can be made early in the merger process that will minimize culture clash problems, facilitate the optimum integration of the two cultures, and greatly increase the probability of success of the merger.

DUE DILIGENCE AND LEGAL RESTRICTIONS

We have made the case for performing a proper and thorough Cultural Due Diligence. However, there are some very real issues of legality and practicality that must be worked out before proceeding. While thorough qualitative research methodologies, including observation, interviews, and focus groups, are necessary, these activities cannot actually happen in most instances until *after* the decision has been made to make a particular acquisition and the letter of intent or acceptance has been issued.

Prior to this, access to the people working in the target company is usually limited to a few key executives—and occasionally a few specifically identified individual key contributors. This means that the exquisite detail that is necessary for development of a full and proper integration plan will not be available until *after* the final selection of the company to merge with or purchase has been made.

While this may seem to be a serious constraint, it actually parallels other aspects of the due diligence process. Full financial and legal due diligence also cannot occur until after a letter of intent or acceptance. While the financial books of a company can be reviewed and scrutinized earlier, actual verification of inventory, work in process, outstanding orders, and accounts payable must wait.

The same situation exists in terms of Cultural Due Diligence. A *high-level assessment of the broad cultural variables* of the target organization can be done early in the process and can be one of the inputs into the decision as to which of a number of possible companies is going to be the target for merger or acquisition. But it will be an informed guess at best.

PRE LETTER OF INTENT/ACCEPTANCE ACTIVITIES

Four critical things can be done prior to a letter of intent that can have considerable value to the acquirer's M&A team: (1) a self-assessment by the acquirer, if it hasn't already been done; (2) a high-level estimate of the probable cultural characteristics of potential target companies to estimate the probable level of difficulty of integration; (3) an assessment of potential compatibility with target company executive teams; and (4) detailed information that can be used to recommend retention strategies for key people at the target companies.

Know Thyself First

The first piece of useful information is a detailed analysis of the culture of the acquiring company. Obviously, without this data there is no baseline to compare with the characteristics of the target companies. But in our experience, very few companies have this information current and available at the level of detail necessary.

A cultural self-assessment in and of itself will usually have clear benefits for the acquiring company. First, it is not unusual for this activity to surface what will become "time critical" issues—things that are not going all that well internally, have not been dealt with, and are not desirable to take forward into a merged operation. Further, there may well be areas within the acquiring company that are less than supportive of an acquisition in general and/or strong negative impressions of particular companies that may be in the pool of potential targets.

Knowing this in advance enables the acquirer to engage in any necessary pre-merger work internally. Time spent uncovering and resolving issues is time saved in the crucial and time-sensitive integration period.

Know Thy Target

In order to accomplish the second possible pre-letter CDD activity, high-level assessment of the target organization's culture, a very detailed review of any documents that could give an indication of that organization's culture is in order. These include the annual report, advertising, public statements of mission, vision, strategy and values, employee and customer satisfaction surveys, newsletters, the organization's website and intranet, and so forth. It is also wise at this point to compare notes with others, such as legal and financial, for any cultural indicators that they may have picked up while doing their own preliminary due diligence.

Additional sources of cultural information usually include any documented policies and procedures, organizational charts and job descriptions, and things like training and orientation materials, if any. Other items of interest are any HR-related information that may be available, such as employee retention data, employee relations data on grievances, recruitment standards, and any general demographic data on the employee population. Things like job titles, attitude or climate survey data, age spread and tenure data, and such can all help inform the acquirer about the target organization's probable culture and how well it may fit with the acquirer's culture.

Executive Team Compatibility

Determining the probable compatibility of the executives and senior managers of the acquiring and target companies is next. This is usually accomplished informally over a series of visits, meetings, and social events in the Pre Letter period. Executives of both companies will get to know one another, size each other up, and form impressions. Opinions will be formed on both sides as to how compatible they will be and the degree to which they will be able to work together.

Obviously, not all executives will remain in place within the new organization, due to functional redundancy. No organization needs two CEOs, marketing directors, or finance directors, but it is dangerous and arrogant to assume that the executives of the acquiring company or companies driving the merger will stay and that those of the target company will go. Who stays and who goes should be a careful and objective decision, based on the business needs of the new organization. In this Pre Letter phase, general compatibility and ability of the executive teams of both organizations can be assessed, and as a rule the more compatible the executives the better.

Retention of Key People

Early on, it is possible to identify and interview key people in the target company who should be the focus of retention strategies that will see them stay with and continue to contribute to the new organization. This requires a series of very intensive interviews with the executives and any key employees who have been identified. Key people are often individual contributors, such as scientists, technical experts, or subject-matter experts—often world-class experts—who make very valuable and continuing contributions to the organization.

Interviews with key people should be friendly and cordial and reflect a real interest in the person's expertise and contribution. The basic purpose of the interview is to get to know the key person and to determine what he or she values about the current organization that, if lost, might make him or her look elsewhere.

A sample key person interview is shown in Exhibit 4.2.

Information obtained about key executives and individual contributors can be used to begin planning retention strategies so that they will remain with, and contribute to, the new organization. All too often retention strategy is limited to various forms of "golden handcuffs," specific financial payouts based on staying with the company for a specified period of time. The track record of these approaches is spotty at best, even in terms of retaining the people just for the required period of time. Truly valuable people tend to be equally or more valuable to other companies—especially the competition—and matching a retention payoff with a signing bonus is not difficult. The greatest problem with financial incentives is that you often keep the "body" on the job but the brain and heart—which make the person a "key" person—may well check out long before the retention period ends.

Retention policies must be designed to appeal to the very things that attracted people to the company in the first place. The key drivers for high-performing people staying with a particular company are rarely purely financial. They are almost always the characteristics of the job and working environment, coupled with

Exhibit 4.2. Sample Key Person Interview

PERSONAL

1. Schooling, employment history, family, and hobbies?
2. Career progression since joining this company?
3. Personal values (family, profession, community, and so on)?
4. International experience (employment, schools, and travel)?
5. How do you manage the balance between company needs and individual needs?
6. What are the particular skills and abilities you bring to this job?

PROFESSIONAL

7. Two greatest successes with the company. Why and how accomplished?
8. Two greatest failures or disappointments. Why and what was learned?
9. Who was the best boss you ever had? What made it so good?
10. What was the greatest job you ever had? What made it so good?
11. What is your functional responsibility?
12. What are your key priorities?
13. What do you value most in your peers, subordinates, boss, customers?
14. If applicable, how would your subordinates describe your management style? Your peers? Your boss?

THE COMPANY

15. What is the company's overall strategy?
16. How does your function relate to the overall company strategy?
17. What are this company's strengths? Weaknesses? Threats? Opportunities?
18. How does this management team work in relation to decision making? Contention? Candor? Conflict?
19. As this merger or acquisition proceeds, what are the key things from this company that you want to be sure to bring forward? What are the key things you would just as soon leave behind?
20. What are the key things the companies need to keep in mind to assure success as this acquisition proceeds?
21. Who are some of the heroes of this company? What are some of the legends and lore of the company?
22. How would you describe the current morale in the company? In your function?
23. What is this company's competitive edge and how is it maintained?
24. What do you value most about the company? About your job?

personal needs and desires, which play a prominent role as well. Key person interviews, done in the manner described, can provide the best information for how to retain the talent.

Additionally, these key person interviews will add considerable detail to the high-level estimate of the target company culture.

ASSESSING DEGREE OF DIFFICULTY OF CULTURAL INTEGRATION

From a preliminary assessment of (1) the target company's culture, (2) the relative compatibility of the executive teams, and (3) the number of key people within the target company and ways to retain them, it is possible to make a preliminary estimate of the resources required to integrate the two companies and how difficult it will be. Cultural characteristics, such as the comparative degree of formality, balance of control versus support, internal versus external focus, decision-making processes, cross-functional styles and patterns, team versus individual accountability, and so forth, should also come out of this preliminary analysis.

While this information is not sufficient for writing a detailed description of the actual operating culture of the target company or for developing a proper integration plan, in most cases, it can be used to compare several potential target companies in terms of degree of potential integration difficulty. Further, the information can serve to inform the design of the eventual full Cultural Due Diligence to be performed later, thus greatly accelerating the integration process.

GETTING IT RIGHT—THE HEWLETT-PACKARD/COMPAQ MERGER

One year after approval and implementation of the Hewlett-Packard/Compaq Computer merger, it certainly looks like a winner, as does HP's CEO and primary force behind the merger, Carly Fiorina. Twelve months earlier, HP was very much under siege because of Fiorina's announced intent to acquire Compaq—at war with the Hewlett and Packard families and suffering strong criticism in the business press, on Wall Street, and from its own employees due to the planned $19 billion merger—the largest and most complex in the history of the computer industry. Opponents of the merger, foremost among them Walter Hewlett, the son of HP co-founder Bill Hewlett, led a bitter proxy fight to block the deal. When he lost in a close shareholder vote, he accused HP of buying the votes of large institutional shareholders and sued the company. The suit was dismissed by the

Delaware Chancery Court in 2002, removing the last of many obstacles to the merger. HP and Compaq began operating as "the new hp" in May 2002.

One year later, the *San Francisco Chronicle* (May 4, 2003) detailed some of the early indicators of the merger's success:

- On target to cut approximately $3.1 billion in costs, a year ahead of HP's initial forecast of $2.5 billion by the end of the fiscal year;
- Holding its own in the slumping PC industry and running a close second to Dell Computer, despite early warnings that acquiring Compaq would hurt HP's industry position;
- Revenue and operating profits up;
- Gaining market share in areas such as basic servers; and
- Integration of the two companies ahead of schedule and will conclude a year ahead of schedule.

Hardly the "slow-motion collision of two garbage trucks" predicted by competitor Sun Microsystems CEO Scott McNealy prior to the merger!

Through it all, Carly Fiorina remained publicly unflappable, providing a case study in leadership under pressure. Since joining HP in 1999, Fiorina had made some high-profile and controversial decisions—none more controversial than her treatment of the beloved "HP Way," the bedrock of the company's culture.

In a speech for the Wharton Leadership Lecture Series and reported in the *Wharton Journal News* (March 24, 2003), Fiorina shared what she saw as the negative impact that the HP Way, largely credited for driving its unprecedented growth from its humble beginnings in a garage in Palo Alto, California, in 1938, was having on the company's current culture and way of doing things. Her analysis showed that HP had missed earnings projections for nine quarters in a row, while 75 percent of the employees were rated as "exceeding expectations" in their performance reviews over the same period. She found that proposed innovations and new ideas were being shot down because they were "not the HP Way" and that it had, in essence, become a shield against new ideas.

Fiorina decided that the HP culture needed a shake-up and worked with the executive committee to develop and introduce Cultural Cornerstones for the New HP, consisting of company values and corporate objectives that are aligned with and supportive of HP's strategies, structure and processes, metrics and rewards, policies and procedures, and behaviors. She also revamped the performance measures and emphasized developing managers with cross-functional expertise.

Given this evidence of Fiorina's cultural and system awareness, perhaps stemming from her degree in medieval history and certainly influenced by her leadership of Lucent's IPO and spinoff from AT&T, it should come as no surprise that she insisted on Cultural Due Diligence and comprehensive integration planning in conjunction with the Compaq merger. Well ahead of the merger's approval, she assembled an elite team that studied past mergers in the computer and technology industry to learn from their mistakes. Their research underscored the importance of a unified organizational culture and of speed in the integration process.

We participated in the design and implementation of HP's Cultural Due Diligence, which consisted of extensive executive interviews, focus groups, site observations, and document reviews. All of the CDD data was summarized and fed into HP's integration engine—the "Clean Room"—where up to 650 cultural consultants, working part-time while continuing their regular jobs, planned the implementation of integration initiatives.

While many other factors are responsible for the apparent success of the merger, *Cultural Due Diligence and integration planning played a major role.* As an example, HP appointed its top three levels of executives before the deal was closed, greatly accelerating the filling of other management levels, which is typically a slow and drawn-out process that lowers the morale of both managers and staff.

In summary, it certainly appears that Fiorina and HP got it right. When mergers go wrong, it happens relatively quickly and is very obvious within the first year. This one is ahead of schedule after the first year. That reality alone makes it one of the most successful mergers in the industry, regardless of what the market may or may not do in the future to this combination.

We'll discuss more about doing Cultural Due Diligence in the next chapter.

Performing Cultural Due Diligence

A S ANY SOUND ORGANIZATIONAL RESEARCH SHOULD, a CDD process employs both qualitative and quantitative data collection. The *quantitative* methodology involves survey forms with numerical ratings (usually employing a five-point or seven-point semantic differential scale) in regard to predetermined domains or characteristics of the culture. Here's how the process works.

THE CDD PROCESS

Qualitative methodology utilizes interviews, focus groups, workplace observations, and documentation review, with the researchers capturing the voice of the culture and the people through collecting verbatim responses and organizing the data either according to predetermined cultural attributes or according to the areas in which the cultural behaviors are exhibited.

Quantitative methods utilized are informed by and based on early capture of high-level qualitative data by means of CEO/Executive interviews, workplace observation, and documentation review. An initial web-based CDD survey is developed and administered to a sample of the total population of the two organizations engaged in the merger to develop high-level cultural profiles of each organization.

The survey data is then used to plan and conduct a subsequent round of interviews and focus groups with a weighted sample of managers across the business units and geography of both organizations. A subsequent web-based CDD survey is developed based on this and the initial survey data, and the survey is administered to everyone in the combined organizations if desired.

Ultimately, in addition to the CDD surveys, we interview key managers, starting with the CEOs, executive teams, and all essential senior managers, moving on to a targeted sample of middle managers and supervisors. We supplement this by selected focus groups, workplace observations, and documentation review.

Typically, the data is organized and presented within the following cultural domains, previously presented in Chapter 4.

1. Intended Direction and Results

Ascertain, from the top of the organization on down, what the company intends to accomplish. What is the business plan about, what is the strategic intent and purpose of the organization, what results are expected from the business activity of the organization, and, most importantly, how are these things talked about, described, and communicated level by level?

This one area alone can yield very telling data about the "way things are done around here." For example, most of the airline industry is very overt about the importance of customer service and satisfying customer needs. At the boardroom level, and generally at the senior executive level, this is clearly understood as an issue of competitive position and repeat business.

Yet, when you talk to the people on the plane, at check-in, and in the airline club, the definition of customer service and customer satisfaction can take on some interesting nuances. For example, on one major carrier the cabin crew will first note that their "real job" is safety, with the "service" aspects a clear second; in fact, when the "service" part of the flight commences, passengers are usually asked to stay in their seats and not get in the way. On another carrier, passengers are immediately encouraged to make their wishes known as "the crew is here to make your flight as pleasant and comfortable as possible."

When asked about efforts to improve customer satisfaction, the former carrier's staff talk about the money being spent on upgrading meals, decor of the aircraft, enlarged lounges, and other physical aspects the airline is providing; the latter carrier's staff talk about the passenger "experience" and their part in assuring the customer is "satisfied enough to choose us again next time," with a clear emphasis on the interpersonal service provided. One focuses on equipment and the other on attitude as the key components in customer satisfaction—both valid, but very different.

A convincing case can be made for either approach, but imagine the differing views and arguments that could ensue down through the ranks if these two carriers merged, even though both clearly value customer satisfaction and service as key elements of their business plans.

2. Key Measures

Find out what the company measures, why, and what happens as a result. The key measures say a lot about the manner in which the company and its executives and staff are driven, particularly when the consequences for each measure are considered.

When a large company investigated why its initiative to enhance customer service and employee retention was not providing any results, a big part of the answer was in the key measures domain. When the store managers' supervisors reviewed results with the store managers, only inventory control, paperwork, and dollar volume received real focus. These areas were not only measured, but had consequences to both parties for success or failure. There was only a "nice job" comment for service and retention improvement. Since all parties had their hands very full, if not overloaded, with the "standard key measures," there was no time for the "add-on" stuff. Especially in the current times of lean staff, most people, particularly in management/supervisory positions, are extremely busy. The focus will always be on what they perceive as truly important. They will try to avoid the perceived consequences of failure, so key measures and their consequences must be examined.

3. Key Business Drivers

Check out the primary issues driving the business strategy. Is the focus on competitive edge and, if so, how is that defined—price differentiation, quality, market share, service, reliability, or what?

This tells you how the company views its industry and its subsequent efforts within the industry. If one company defines success in terms of total market share while another defines theirs as net profit margin, there is considerable room for disagreement about which actions are appropriate to correct unacceptable results or when deciding on suitable new product offerings.

4. Infrastructure

How is the company organized? What are the company's policies and procedures? What is the nature of the reporting relationships? How do the staff systems interface with the line systems? What is the nature of the relationships among groups and units in the organization?

For example, are people expected to "go directly to whomever you need to talk to," or must proprieties be observed between different levels or functions. Are business units supposed to drive their business priorities first and foremost and respond to corporate, staff, or other unit needs when convenient, or are they supposed to assure that they are responsive to corporate needs and check with other units to assure there are no conflicts or unexpected impacts?

5. Organizational Practices

Find out the formal and informal systems in place and what part they play in daily life while doing the work. How much flexibility is allowed at what levels in which systems? What is the relationship between political reality and business reality?

For example, how are budgets developed and managed? When Westinghouse bought CBS, significant disagreement occurred over what were and were not "reasonable" expenses, particularly when it came to entertainment budgets. These disagreements resulted in dramatic upheaval.

Besides formal systems such as budgeting, this area includes how staff groups such as Legal, Human Resources, Public Relations, Purchasing, General Services, and such are accessed and utilized by line units and by one another. It is not unusual to find that a particular person or function is considered sacrosanct, regardless of the impact the person or function may be having on important business issues. It's not uncommon to hear something like "You don't dare question the people in Legal [or Finance or Information Management, or some other (usually staff) function]." These people or functions are considered "above" the routine of accomplishing the business of the company. In common parlance, these areas or people are generally referred to as political bases of power, which are separate from or above the overall corporate structure.

6. Leadership/Management Practices

See what the balance is between leadership and management approaches with staff. What basic value systems about employees are in place? How are people treated and why? How is the business plan implemented through the management system? How are decisions made? Who is involved in what, and when?

There are clear behavioral differences between management and leadership functions, and clearly both are important in running a successful business. The issue is to find which approach is predominant in each area/department of the company. This domain relates primarily to the middle management group, but has obvious impact on the next domain.

7. Supervisory Practices

Investigate the dynamics involved in overseeing the performance of work. Supervisory practices have a major impact on employees' feelings about the company and the work they do. The nature of the interaction between the employee and the immediate supervisor is one of the primary climate-setters for the culture of the company.

For example, at one company, supervisors were expected to be curt and aggressive with important issues; speaking softly meant the topic could safely be ignored. The same abrupt behaviors in another company could conceivably be considered rude and abusive.

8. Work Practices

Observe how the actual work is performed. Is the emphasis on individual responsibility or group responsibility? What degree of control, if any, does the individual worker have on the work flow, quality, rate, tools utilized, and supplies needed?

A classic example to illustrate this is in manufacturing, where two companies are making the same products but one allows any worker to stop the production line at any time he or she deems it necessary. This latter company views the individual worker as in the best position to recognize a defective product. The other company does not allow unauthorized line stoppages. Instead, only the manager, who has the knowledge of overall production needs, can assess whether a stoppage is worth the lost production. Obviously, these are two very different, yet potentially appropriate, ways of viewing the same issue.

9. Technology Use

Check out the company's technology base and how technology is used. This must be considered in relation to both internal systems and equipment, as well as the services and products provided to customers. How current is the technology being utilized? What are people used to in relation to technological support/resources?

For example, conflicts and confusion may occur if a company that is firmly grounded in computer e-mail procedures merges with a company in which individual computers are not generally available. Discussions of high-tech versus low-tech approaches to many aspects of running a business can quickly descend into accusations of "Luddites" opposing "techno-geeks" when the parties have differing experience and comfort with a given technology.

10. Physical Environment

See how the workplace settings differ. Open work spaces versus private offices, high security versus open access, buildings, furniture, grounds—all can have a bearing on how people feel about work and the company. Changes in these areas, particularly if they are perceived as arbitrary, can result in bad feelings for years.

Imagine, for example, two clients with contradictory approaches, both based on valuing people and increasing productivity. The first company says, "We value people and know that an open office increases interactions and camaraderie, making for happier and more productive workers." The second company states, "We value people, and private work spaces aid in the thought processes, enabling greater focus and increased productivity."

11. Perceptions and Expectations

Ask how people expect things to happen. What do they believe is important? What do they think should be important, versus what they perceive the company feels is important?

In resolving a union/management dispute in a plant in jeopardy of being closed, we found it was necessary to deal first with the conviction in union ranks that management was a revolving door occupied by short-timers who did not care about the plant or the community. This was matched by management's equally strong belief that the employees and unions did not care about the products, the competition, or the plant's profitability. Both beliefs were untrue, yet both parties were so sure of their perceptions that they never discussed them with the other party. These strongly held beliefs (perceptions) were at the core of their inability to work together.

12. Cultural Indicators and Artifacts

Observe how people dress and address one another. What is the match between formal work hours and actual hours spent working? What company-sponsored activities exist and what are they like?

Company picnics and social clubs can be seen as major tools in pulling people together and building a family atmosphere or as impositions on employees' personal and family time, generating friction and resentment. Once again, two different companies in the same business and similar social/geographical settings can see things completely differently.

These twelve domains cover the major components of corporate culture. However, at least two areas commonly mentioned in discussions of corporate culture should not be overlooked—*values and beliefs and myths, legends, and heroes.* In actuality, these are imbedded in the twelve domains. By digging into each domain, underlying values and beliefs can be uncovered. This is far more effective than simply asking, "What are the values and beliefs around here?" That type of inquiry generally results in puzzled looks.

The same is true of myths, legends, and heroes. These are simply the "stories" or anecdotal versions that give more direct and immediate meaning to the belief systems operating in the company. Myths, legends, and heroes will present themselves as the twelve domains are examined, especially through use of qualitative data-gathering techniques.

In accumulating corporate cultural data, the most useful information comes from qualitative processes—primarily *interviews, focus groups, and observation.* Information gathered in this manner is rich in anecdotes and examples of how the culture is acted out and talked about. Stories give personal meaning to the culture and provide examples and demonstrations that are easy for people in the target culture to relate with.

These anecdotes and stories enable those doing culture modification to engage in dialogue about work issues in a direct manner. A rich trove of stories and examples, derived directly from the target cultures, makes these discussions much easier and makes their relevance to the business needs and individual behavior much more obvious. Without rich and abundant qualitative data, the organizational change process becomes much more difficult, all the way from design through implementation.

In our discussion of the twelve domains, we provided examples of very different approaches to each. There was no "right" or "wrong" way; the approaches were simply different and equally valid ways of dealing with the same cultural phenomenon. This sort of difference is often the basis from which culture clash can arise; however, in our experience, the probability of having two cultures that cannot be effectively merged, given the willingness to invest sufficient time and resources, is highly unlikely—but some are obviously easier to merge than others.

CULTURAL ASSESSMENT

Cultural assessment (this process is shown in the entire top portion of Figure I.1 on page 3) is essentially the comparison of data and information about the cultures of the two companies involved in the merger or acquisition in order to determine the relative degree of difficulty and effort that will be required in aligning and integrating them. Most of the data and information will come from the CDD performed on each of the companies, organized for comparison into the twelve cultural domains or in some other consistent and logical way.

At this point, cultural indicators that may have surfaced in the other due diligence activities should be identified and included in the assessment. For example, the people doing legal due diligence may have picked up a pattern of employee lawsuits against the company or problems with customers or suppliers. The financial due diligence may have revealed a pattern of frequent Workers' Compensation and disability claims, or an unusually high number of temporary employees working for extended periods of time. These may well be cultural indicators meriting further investigation.

All of the data is consolidated and analysed, resulting in a draft of a high-level Cultural Integration Plan for discussion with the CEO and executive committee, after which will come subsequent revision and a final document.

As a partial example of a side-by-side comparison of two organizational cultures, a Focus Group Summary Report is presented in Exhibit 5.1.

Exhibit 5.1. Sample Focus Group Summary

This summary is based on the data gathered by Vector Group in fifty-three focus groups (thirty-two within Company A and twenty-one within Company B) in ten different countries, in business units and locations specified by Company A and Company B coordinators. The focus groups ranged in size from six to fifteen people, meaning that approximately five hundred managers and staff members of the two companies were involved in this activity. The people attending these groups were randomly selected and invited to participate.

The data sample is too small to be definitive in terms of location-by-location detail, although some general regional trends are clear. The data sample is more than sufficient for a high-level overview and specification of company-wide characteristics of both companies.

The major focus group findings fall into four categories:

1. *The Merger*—both companies' views/opinions about the impending merger.
2. *Culture*—with both companies in flux and searching for who they were, who they are, and what the culture of the desired new company will be.
3. *Organizational Change*—with both companies struggling with large-scale change activities that have not been successfully assimilated and, in the case of Company A, that are being resisted.
4. *Leadership*—with both companies facing severe internal and external problems that have surfaced within the last two years, the spotlight has been on the leadership of both companies as it has responded to these problems and challenges.

THE MERGER

Company B focus group participants say that its staff view the merger as a great opportunity. Company A was never the "enemy" and is a respected name—and a company that seems to know how to execute a strategy. They report that people feel the merger is an opportunity to regain the lead in the industry.

Company A focus group participants describe the merger as a potential step down in both profitability and in stature and prestige. A large number of the focus group participants seem to feel that Company A is somehow being sullied by "getting in bed" with what they consider a company of dubious ethics and reputation and apparently desperate to merge in order to survive.

(Continued)

Exhibit 5.1. Sample Focus Group Summary (Continued)

When examining the generally reported reactions of staff to the intended mergers, it is a curious to note that Company B employees are acting and sounding more like the *acquiring* company—bold, positive, and energetic—while Company A employees are acting more like the *acquired* company—reticent, negative, and lethargic. Company B focus group participants reported looking forward to the merger and wanting to get on with it, while the Company A focus group participants were very vocal about what they perceive they will lose and were expressing nostalgia backwards to what they consider "the good old days."

Focus group participants in both companies reported that they are not well-informed about the planned merger—especially the rationale or business case for it. Both groups lack clarity on the vision of the new company and on the timeframe of the merger and any planned integration activities. Company B's people are not overly concerned about their lack of information, stating that they "just want to get on with it"—to make it happen. Company A's people are not happy with their lack of information—which they view as a reiteration of the talking points that they have heard before. A significant number wondered why the only passion for the merger exhibited at the executive level was by the two CEOs and why the other executive members were not providing similar strong endorsements of the merger.

CULTURE

From what was reported in the focus groups, Company B has a strong tactical task orientation but lacks clearly stated direction or a long-term strategy—other than to beat the competition. Company B participants report a strong "can do" attitude, and the people in the focus groups feel almost anything is possible given a clear task and minimum time to deliver. They say their tendency is to act quickly and to take corrective action, if necessary, on the fly.

The focus group participants said that Company B is very entrepreneurial and focused on making things happen, but has reportedly become so caught up in internal change, reorganization, and redirection that its people are unsure of just what it is they are supposed to be doing. The focus group participants appeared to be an energized group, champing at the bit to get moving, but appear to have no plan. For the most part, they reportedly don't really care just what the plan is as long as they have one and can get on with it. The problem, as they report it, is that the industry is in major transition and they need a new strategy and aren't getting one. Customer focus is a strong element of the Company B culture, and the customer and the competition were clearly on the

Exhibit 5.1. **(Continued)**

participants' minds, as was the reported continuing erosion of the company's current position in the marketplace.

The Company A focus group participants said that Company A has a strong identity and sense of purpose that they perceive as being under attack from within. They reported that the restructured organization is not effective and is not well-received by the company's people. Their report characterized the general cultural pattern as consensus-based, requiring that its people must *"be sure of what you are doing and involve all parties"* before taking action. They term themselves as lacking openness and candor in their interactions and as being fed up with the current glacial pace of decision making. They hope that a merger with Company B, whom they perceive to be quick and decisive, will speed up the their pace of getting things done.

The Company A focus group participants said they are no longer sure of what they are supposed to be doing and just what the future is supposed to be. In their view, a vision, purpose, and a clear strategic plan must precede effective action. As reported, it would appear that this is a company that has not allowed the analysis and resulting clarity that the culture demands to occur and percolate down through the organization as it used to do.

CHANGE MANAGEMENT

As reported by the focus groups, both companies are in the midst of unresolved major changes that are creating significant degrees of dissonance and internal focus. But the nature of the unresolved changes and their solution are remarkably different in the two companies. Throughout Company B, people freely stated in the focus groups that there are several as-yet unassimilated acquisitions—which continue to create tensions and undermine cross-functional effectiveness.

Loyalty seems to be more to a unit or area than to the company as a whole. When looking at the data from the focus groups, it is clear that, the further away from head office, the more pronounced these subcultures become, though they are also reportedly alive and well at the head office as well.

From the abundant comments in the focus groups, it appears that Company A has unresolved angst from the sale of a major unit of the company and a redirected strategy and infrastructure that is neither understood nor accepted. Loyalty is reportedly deep and strong toward the company, but the employees in the focus groups were not sure just what and who the company is anymore. They seemed to clearly understand

(Continued)

Exhibit 5.1. Sample Focus Group Summary (Continued)

that they are no longer the old Company A, but lack agreement or even common understanding of what they are supposed to be now.

In terms of the changes already instituted and those anticipated to result from the merger, Company A people are focused on what they have lost or think they will lose as a result of the merger, and Company B people are focused on salvation and a successful future as a result of the merger. In our view there is an important subtlety here—Company A is adrift and looking backward with longing, while Company B is adrift but could care less about the past, only wanting to survive, prosper, and be on top again with a new and better business plan.

LEADERSHIP

Review of the focus group data indicates a strong perception that both companies have encountered an evolving leadership crisis over the last two years, but the crisis takes on a different form in each of the companies.

In Company B the focus group data show that there is a loss of faith in senior management, which generally refers to the people reporting to the CEO but, as reported, does not include the CEO himself. There is a fair amount of positive feeling in the middle management ranks about the next immediate management level and possibly the next level up, coupled with extreme dissatisfaction for the business unit head level and above as a group. It is the senior team—absent the CEO—that gets the bulk of the blame for the current reported environment of stagnation, lack of focus, and poor financial results.

Any overt dissatisfaction with the CEO appears to be focused on the perception that he has not been decisive enough with his team, forcing them to make decisions and stick with them rather than intervene.

In Company A, the focus group data indicate that there is a loss of faith and growing dissatisfaction with their CEO specifically, and that this reported dissatisfaction does not seem to include anyone else in senior management. The CEO seems to be assigned all the perceived management sins in Company A, where there is a relatively strong positive identification with and view of senior management other than the CEO.

The CEO is perceived by those participating in the focus groups to have come in and reportedly changed things with no organizational collaboration—and apparently with no negotiated internal support from his own management team. It could be said that he has attempted to be decisive, but there is no perceived evidence of internal management

Exhibit 5.1. (Continued)

realignment behind the new directions. It is unclear whether he has taken any of the senior management with him in the reorganization.

When it comes to solutions or interventions, while both companies have severe leadership problems, they are fundamentally different and would seem to require different actions and approaches to resolve. As they now stand, both will clearly have a negative impact on making the merger work and on building a strong new company culture, unless resolved.

DRAFTING THE CULTURAL ALIGNMENT AND INTEGRATION PLAN

The cultural assessment portion of the draft Cultural Alignment and Integration Plan that is developed for discussion with top management should include:

- A summary of CDD activities and data sources;
- A summary of the results of the CDD activities, including the employee survey, executive interviews, focus groups, documentation review, and workplace observations;
- Summary profiles of the cultures and subcultures of each company, together with any geographical or cultural differences;
- The key cultural synergies between the companies;
- Areas of probable culture clash between the organizations;
- Opinions about whether the two can be merged to create a new organizational culture; and
- The estimated difficulty of cultural integration and the scope of the time and resources required to accomplish that integration.

By using the type of assessment recommended here, you will specifically address the leading cause of the failure of mergers and acquisitions—*cultural clashes between the two organizations*. Such an assessment also provides detailed information that can be used to develop an efficient and effective Cultural Integration Plan to address the second major cause of failure—*lack of speed in integration*.

Cultural Alignment and Integration

PART 3 OF THIS BOOK consists of five chapters:

The first three of these chapters focus on and provide a walkthrough of the Cultural Integration Process Flowchart, shown in Figure I.3, which details the activities in the process. The focus of this cultural alignment and integration effort is the effective modification and merging of the two companies' cultures into a new organizational culture that supports implementation of the new business plan.

These chapters will not deal with other activities of organizational integration, such as how best to merge salary plans or benefits of the two companies, combine

Figure I.3. Cultural Integration Process Flowchart

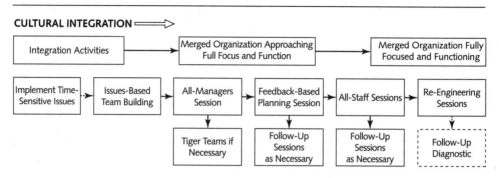

their IT systems, and so forth. Rather, we will discuss cultural integration—bringing the cultures of the two organizations involved in the merger or acquisition together to define "how we do things" in the new organization and gaining support of and commitment to the new organization's business plan from the organization's people—especially the executive group and management group charged with implementing the business plan for the new organization.

It is important to keep the issue of integrating post-merger operations in mind, as that integration is a transformational change. This means that the methodologies utilized for linear change and continuous improvement do not generally apply.

The chapters in this section build on the well-researched technology of organizational change management—be it incremental or transformational, participative or declarative—required. Procedures for successfully managing organizational change are presented in Exhibit I.1.

As in any transformational change, managers will require time and support to disengage from old patterns and plan and implement new ways of working. The cultural or value-based "soft" issues of behavior are the real problem in integration, not the strategic or infrastructure "hard" behavioral issues. These are important and complex, but relatively straightforward areas of the integration to achieve. Cultural or value-based patterns of behavior, especially those exhibited by the organization's executives and managers, are where significant culture clash issues often arise.

Exhibit I.1. General Considerations for Change Management

When considering change management in organizations, a number of issues need to be considered prior to selecting any particular method or approach. A number of these factors are, unfortunately, not dealt with by many conventional approaches or consulting firms. To begin with, it is inappropriate to consider the change topic simply as a project to be managed. The reality of the global business climate today and into the foreseeable future is that change is endemic.

For years, the basic models of change always included an underlying three-step foundation of change management that was described by Kurt Lewin as:

1. Unfreeze the current organization/system/function.
2. Institute the change.
3. Re-freeze the organization/system/function.

The real problem today is with a literal application of the last principle in particular, and the subsequent implications with the first principle when going forward into the next major change. Let us deal with these by beginning with the third principle. When taken literally, it goes beyond the simple issue of making sure the change is fully implemented and maintained. It has built into it an implication that "change" is now done with.

How practical is this assumption in the fast-evolving technical and competitive environments of today? Industry after industry is finding itself in the position of "continuous change." The phrase itself has become a watchword of any quality system—and quality systems are now applied to far more than just the manufacturing environments where they were first born. They are now a critical element of most retail and service sector businesses as well.

Modern conventional business wisdom is that stability or stasis (lack of change in business) equals decay and eventual death. Customer expectations are changing constantly; standards are constantly rising. Technology is constantly evolving, and competition is ever more omnipresent and global. How can one marry any implication of stability with the current environment?

To be practical, the elements of change management related to assuring that the change is truly implemented and sticks until the next "major" change (see below) should be incorporated into the second principle, instituting the change. Further, while instituting the change, you must include the concepts of "continuous improvement" in most instances. This will provide resilience in the face of future change.

(Continued)

Exhibit I.1. General Considerations for Change Management (Continued)

INCREMENTAL AND TRANSFORMATIONAL CHANGE

This leads us to another major principle of change management that many current models do not take into account. Today change is considered to fall into two major categories: *incremental* or *continuous* and *transformational* or *major*.

While transformational change does still have, at least on the surface, many of the elements of program management that look and feel like the old traditional models, there is still the major shift of ending in a position of going forward—not being re-frozen.

Incremental or continuous change is dramatically different. This must become part and parcel of ongoing management. At this level, change management is a fundamental management skill much like planning, budgeting, and supervising. It is a daily requirement of routine management at all levels.

PARTICIPATIVE AND DECLARATIVE CHANGE

Now let's look at the last major shift in change management today—the need for speed. This was always around, but has increased exponentially, increasing the focus on participation in change versus change directed from above. Not all change is or is even capable of being participative in nature. While participative change is considered ideal, problems with it are two-fold:

1. Many changes, such as regulatory changes, are by definition not a participative event. They are simply decreed and are binding. Often these required changes include penalties for delay or failure to implement within given time frames. Further, many of these changes dictate the operational detail of the changes as well as the end result. Clearly, they are not "participative" in nature.
2. To properly involve all those impacted by any change carries an implication of time spent in the planning stage, which obviously goes up with the numbers of people involved. Also, participation in the design and planning of the change assumes that all parties know or have access to the information and knowledge necessary to enable intelligent discussion and decision making. Again, this requires time, especially when a change impacts large numbers of people.

In the rapidly moving and highly competitive business world of today, time is of the essence. The speed with which a company can plan and implement necessary change is one of the key factors of maintaining a competitive edge. This does not bode well for many large-scale change efforts being done in a participative mode.

Exhibit I.1. (Continued)

FUNDAMENTALS OF CHANGE

So what principles of change can companies lean on that will increase the success of their change efforts? There are four fundamental principles that apply: (1) *increase the clarity:* that is, fully explain all changes and provide resources and support to aid in this understanding and provide answers to ongoing questions about the change in a timely and supportive manner; (2) *diminish the uncertainty:* this relates to things that are peripheral to the change effort but might be associated with it which often means being equally specific about things not being affected by this particular change; (3) *enhance the benefit* by making sure all parties understand what's in it for them; and (4) *diminish the effort,* which means making the implementation of the change as easy as possible for all those on the receiving end.

The demands on the instigators and planners of change get quite high if the actual change is to be as easy as possible for those on the receiving end of the effort. An often overlooked corollary to this "diminish the effort" concept is to make *not* changing more difficult than changing.

Aligning and Integrating the Executive Group

We assume at this point that a target company has been selected and that the merger or acquisition is going to happen. Cultural due diligence and assessment activities have been completed on both organizations involved. It is now necessary to plan the integration of the two organizational cultures to deal with all problems and issues revealed by the cultural due diligence—and to accomplish this cultural integration as rapidly as possible.

Cultural integration (shown in the bottom half of Figure I.1) is an essential factor in implementing the new organization's business plan and gaining support for and commitment to the plan and to the new organization rapidly from the organization's people.

PLANNING CULTURAL ALIGNMENT AND INTEGRATION

Any integration of two or more organizations to create one effective entity is, in terms of its details, very unique. No two organizations, even in the same industry segment, are alike in their organizational functioning and internal culture.

Therefore, there is no standard textbook integration plan complete with all the necessary elements and details for every possibility. Every integration must be dealt with and adjusted on the basis of the data and information generated from the CDD activities and the findings of other due diligence activities. However, there are some broad general patterns that can guide the development and implementation of an effective integration plan.

First should be a listing of those issues that are time-sensitive, such as legal, regulatory, or competitive demands or broad system alignment issues that require resolution early in the integration process to facilitate subsequent actions.

Depending on the individual situation, there may be some very visible, and therefore critical, value-based differences in organizational operations or culture that are now in or could be in actual conflict with each other. Also there may be issues of initial perceptions about the "other" organization that may interfere with people's willingness and/or ability to move ahead while having positive expectations. Finally, it is not terribly unusual for the CDD to have surfaced some operational or infrastructure issues that are considered to be an ongoing problem within the organization.

Resolving them quickly early in the integration process will have a very positive and immediate impact on people's perceptions about the merger or acquisition and on their expectations for the future.

Second, the cultural integration plan should detail the systematic alignment and integration of the two organizations' cultures at the executive, management, and staff levels. Again, while operational detail and specific content will vary widely between different integration efforts, there is an overall pattern to the cultural alignment and integration activity.

For example, it is not unusual for same-functional areas of two organizations to have more in common with each other than they do with the rest of their own organizations. The sales group in the acquiring company may be more like the sales group in the target company than they are like the rest of the functions and departments in their own company, and vice versa. Or the Brazilian operations of the target company may be more like and aligned to the Brazilian operations of the acquiring company than to the rest of their own company. Such considerations must be reflected in the particular content and activities utilized in each step of the alignment process.

ALIGNING THE ORGANIZATION

Integration, particularly in terms of the people, is primarily an issue of organizational alignment. As such, it requires making the mission and vision (statements of organizational intent and purpose) clear and then aligning the governance (power and influence), infrastructure (policies, procedures, internal systems), strategy (goals, objectives, and daily tasks) and the culture (values, practices, and daily behaviors) with the mission and vision in order to achieve desired results.

This is an activity that, for maximum impact and permanence, is best begun with the most senior level of the organization and then progressively rolled down through all levels of the organization. It is interesting to note that the greatest amount of effort and time spent per employee in achieving this alignment is generally at the *top* of the organization and, if done properly, the least amount of time is required per person at the lower levels.

A Nine-Step Alignment and Integration Model is presented in Exhibit 6.1 that can be used as the basis for the activities and sequence of the cultural integration process. The steps correspond to some of the boxes in Figure 6.1 that follows, which is a break-out of Figure I.1 on page 3.

DISCUSSING RESULTS AND RECOMMENDATIONS WITH CEO

We have already taken care of the first few steps in the model, that is, reviewed the business plan and organizational intent; discussed these with the CEO; and completed a CDD and assessment of both companies. At this point it is time to review all the findings of the organizational scan with the senior executive (Step 4 in Exhibit 6.1.), including all broad systemic and alignment issues that require immediate resolution and time-sensitive issues that require immediate resolution before any further cultural integration activities can be initiated. See Figure 6.1, which has the box shaded.

Actual examples of such issues include:

- *A medical instrument manufacturer's public commitment to the release of an innovative new product by the acquiring company prior to its acquisition of another company.* The CDD discovered serious product support problems that required immediate resolution if the new product release was to succeed. Further, these

Exhibit 6.1. Nine-Step Alignment and Integration Model

[*Note:* items *in italics* are variable in length and content depending on the current organizational situation.]

1. Review business plan and overall organizational intent.
2. Discuss with CEO to achieve ringing clarity on organizational intent and business plan.
3. *Complete a CDD and assessment on both acquiring and target companies.*
4. Review results with CEO and plan work sessions with executive group.
5. *Conduct issues-based team-building sessions with executive group of the new organization. Minimum results are clarity and agreement on strategy/business plan and development of a vision and of a set of organizational values to support the business plan.*
6. *Conduct all-managers sessions with all managers in the new organization. Minimum output is clarity on strategy, business plan, vision, and values of the new organization—and an articulation of necessary leadership and management practices to define the values in performance terms.*
   - *If necessary creation of "tiger teams" to investigate and resolve infrastructure issues.*
7. *Conduct feedback-based planning sessions for executives and managers to review past and present performance of self and unit in relation to the vision, mission, strategy, values, and practices and to develop individual action plans for change, improvement, and development.*
   - *Hold follow-up sessions as necessary.*
8. *Conduct all-staff sessions. Minimum output is clarity on strategy, intent, understanding of management activity around infrastructure and feedback, and solicitation of their ideas/suggestions.*
   - *Hold follow-up sessions as necessary.*
9. *Conduct work process re-engineering sessions as needed.*

problems had to be fixed prior to initiating integration with the acquired company.

- *A transportation software company's system for the management of its key accounts.* The CDD showed that confusing and ambiguous priorities were

Figure 6.1. Discussion of CDD Results with CEO

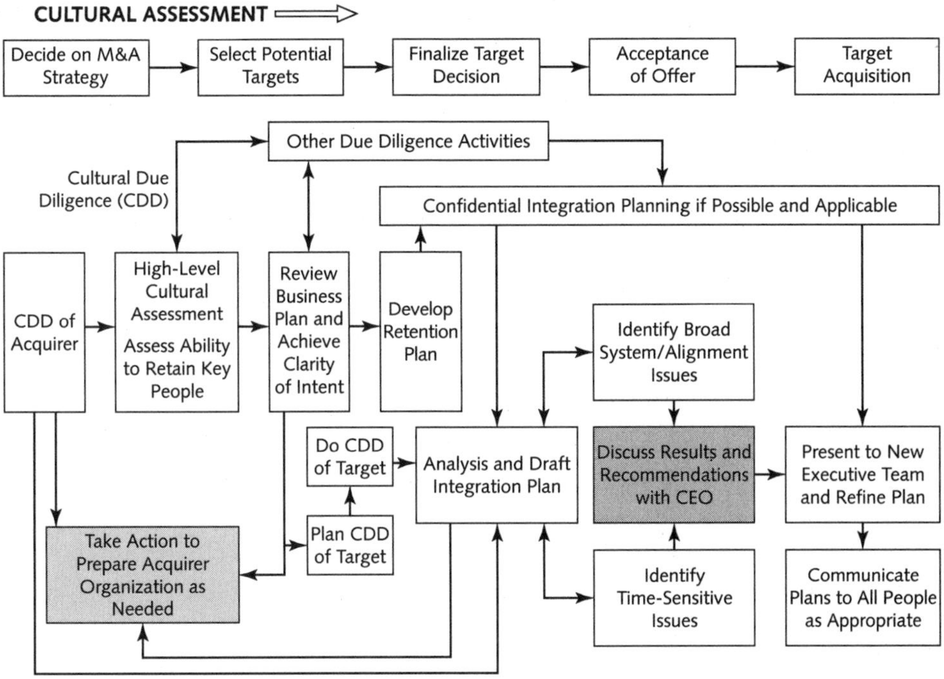

CULTURAL ASSESSMENT ⟹

Decide on M&A Strategy → Select Potential Targets → Finalize Target Decision → Acceptance of Offer → Target Acquisition

Cultural Due Diligence (CDD)

Other Due Diligence Activities

Confidential Integration Planning if Possible and Applicable

CDD of Acquirer → High-Level Cultural Assessment / Assess Ability to Retain Key People → Review Business Plan and Achieve Clarity of Intent → Develop Retention Plan

Identify Broad System/Alignment Issues

Do CDD of Target / Plan CDD of Target → Analysis and Draft Integration Plan → Discuss Results and Recommendations with CEO → Present to New Executive Team and Refine Plan

Take Action to Prepare Acquirer Organization as Needed

Identify Time-Sensitive Issues

Communicate Plans to All People as Appropriate

causing friction between project teams, resulting in inadequate management and support of key accounts and frustration across the project teams, which, if not corrected would result in loss of accounts and revenue, and possible loss of project managers and staff. This problem had to be solved prior to any acquisition or merger effort.

In essence, raising these broad system and time-sensitive issues in the discussion with the CEO and executive committee after the CDD and cultural assessment activities highlights them at the organization's highest level, establishing their priority for resolution.

At this point one would also review the Nine-Step Alignment and Integration Model, with particular focus on Steps 5 through 9 (see Exhibit 6.1). This leads to detailed planning of Step 5—Issues-Based Team Building. While the remainder of the alignment process (Steps 6 through 9) can also be reviewed at this time and most of the content will be known, the steps should be taken one at a time, as

Figure 6.2. Time-Sensitive Issues

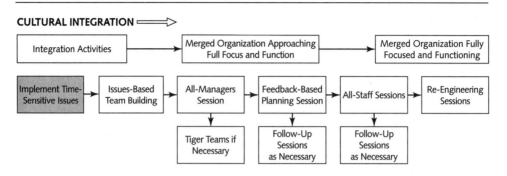

information and experience gained at each step of the process will provide the necessary detail for the next step. We will begin the next chapter with a more detailed discussion of Step 6. Figure 6.2 shows a suggested order for dealing with time-sensitive issues within the larger model.

Time-critical issues and opportunities should be the first activities engaged in by the merged operation. You might say these represent the "low hanging fruit" that can be leveraged for immediate, positive impact.

Once these time-sensitive issues are dealt with, or at least well begun, the alignment needs to follow in very short order.

ALIGNING AND INTEGRATING THE EXECUTIVE GROUP

Now let's turn to the issues of aligning the executive group—the accountable leadership of the organization—and focus on the concepts of mission, vision, strategy, cultural values, and, most importantly, on "walking the talk," or behavioral modeling.

In terms of cultural integration, the most critical aspect of leadership is modeling how they want people around them to act as a result of how they interpret what they observe. The manager's daily behavior is being observed and analyzed, with messages being received both consciously and unconsciously by those who report to him or her. These people in turn pass the messages on down the line, together with their own interpretations of what they expect in terms of actions and behaviors. This process of observation, communication, interpretation, and resulting actions is critical for managers to understand and utilize consciously.

Quite naturally, the more senior the manager, the more critical it becomes to understand and manage this process. However, becoming adept at the process requires a significant degree of self-awareness and considerable introspection—which can be uncomfortable for the best intended of us in the best of situations. In the high-stress situation of a merger integration, modeling can be much more problematic for the executives in question.

Arguably the most critical aspect of leadership and management in a cultural integration effort is the development of a mission, a vision, a strategy, and cultural values for the new organization—the formal statements of organizational direction and intent and process or what it intends to do, and how it intends to do it. The meaningful communication of the mission, vision, strategy, and values throughout the new organization in a manner that minimizes misunderstanding and confusion is vital. A sample of an organization's vision, mission, strategies, and values is presented in Exhibit 6.2.

Exhibit 6.2.   Sample Vision, Mission, Strategy, and Values

1.	Vision	To be the best provider of personal financial advice, services, and solutions—tailored to the individual needs of our customers and their families throughout their lives.
2.	Mission	To improve our cost to revenue ratio from the current .73/1.00 to .55/1.00 by January 1, 2006.
3.	Strategy	Differentiation in the financial services marketplace based on a new and innovative customer proposition: provision of no fee, value-added personal financial advice to our customers and potential customers.
4.	Values	*Customer Focus*—listening to the customer and responding with actions that will make the customer choose us.
		Dependability—meeting our commitments to the customer and to each other by doing what we say we will do.
		Working Together—striving to achieve success through effective collaboration and cooperation across the company.
		Spirit—recognizing and valuing individuals for their innovation, energy, passion, and pride.
		Commercial Awareness—basing our business decisions on the commercial dynamics of our business and industry.

Relatively minor differences among members of the executive team in what they say about the mission, vision, strategies, or values can be perceived and reported as major disagreements three and four levels down in the organization.

The executives and managers of the new organization will need to spend considerable time discussing the concepts of mission, vision, strategy, and values so that they have the same deep understanding of the message and what is intended. This will, in turn, enable them to deliver these messages in a personal yet consistent and cohesive manner across the organization. This takes more then simply agreeing on the written words. Robust discussion will be necessary to achieve the level of understanding and fluency with the concepts that is needed, particularly for good cultural integration.

With these alignment and integration concepts in mind, let's now look at Step 5 of the process shown in Exhibit 6.1.

ISSUES-BASED TEAM BUILDING FOR THE NEW EXECUTIVE TEAM

Issues-Based Team Building is a way to focus on the individual and collective behavior and effectiveness of the new organization's executive team as it provides direction, motivation, guidance, and clarity to the new organization. See Figure 6.3.

In particular, issues-based team building is focused on the directional factors presented in the Organization Alignment Model, a piece of which is shown in Figure 6.4.

Figure 6.3.   Issues-Based Team Building

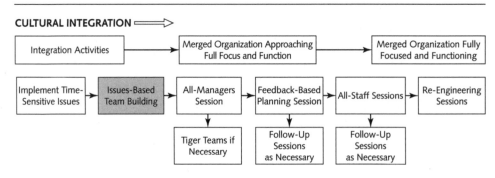

Figure 6.4.   Capstone for the Organizational Alignment Model

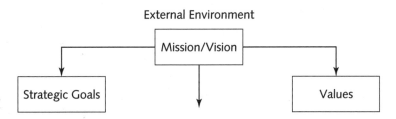

In other words, the executive team must first decide what the mission and vision of the new organization are. They must determine its strategy and strategic goals and its cultural values. They then do the same for the executive team itself.

This determination is the heart of an Issues-Based Team-Building Session. The new executive group must agree on the answers with absolute, ringing clarity before further alignment and integration activities can proceed. In our experience, achieving a basic agreement on these issues takes anywhere from three to five days of intensive work.

This is where extreme candor, together with a relatively deep understanding of the strengths, weaknesses, and personal preferences and style of each member of the team by the other team members, become critical. It is also important to note that this does not necessarily mean a personal "baring of the soul" to each other about all things public and private.

However, it does mean a much more honest appraisal of all aspects that have any bearing on how the team manages and leads and on how they interact with one another. This degree of candor and understanding is not the norm on most senior teams, nor most other teams in business settings for that matter, but it is absolutely critical in the case of post-merger operations.

The term "issues-based" in this step relates both to personal management and leadership style and also to the issues that will have been uncovered during the CDD. Numerous issues of strategy, culture, infrastructure, and real or potential culture clash will have to be resolved as quickly as possible by the executive management team.

It should be pointed out that this step probably requires the use of outside consultants or facilitators. In many circumstances it might not be advisable to utilize internal consultants due to the climate of openness and candor and the confidential nature of the information being discussed.

While this step may well involve a series of follow-on meetings, once there is agreement on the mission, vision, strategy, and cultural values for the new organization, the process can continue with the managers, the subject of the next chapter. A sample statement of values and practices that could come out of such a meeting is presented in Appendix E.

Aligning the Management Group

THE SIXTH STEP IN THE NINE-STEP PROCESS that was shown in Exhibit 6.1 is a meeting, or a series of meetings, which will include all of the managers in the organization. These meetings, termed All-Managers Sessions, usually last at least two days. The purpose is to achieve absolute clarity on the key outputs of the executive issues-based team-building session (the fifth step) discussed in Chapter 6. (See Figure 7.1.)

The management group, ranging from senior managers to first-line supervisors, is the primary driver of organizational behavior. As we have pointed out, day-to-day management behavior is quite possibly the most powerful form of cultural communication and influence in any organization. Therefore, it is important that all managers in the new organization be absolutely clear on and committed to where the organization is, where it is going, why it is going there, and how it will get there.

The All-Managers Session will have a number of elements, and the order and manner in which they are dealt with are as important as, and in some ways even more important than, the content of the messages. This is not to say that the content is not important, but the content alone will not achieve the necessary outcome of the All-Managers Session.

Figure 7.1. All-Managers Sessions

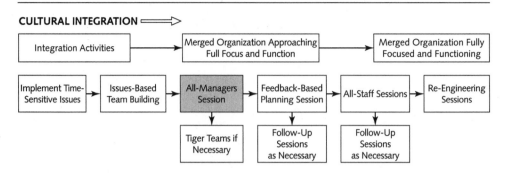

GAINING CLARITY ON ORGANIZATIONAL DIRECTION

There are several basic components in the design of the All-Managers Session. The first is achieving clarity on the current business situation, mission, vision, strategy, and intended cultural values of the new organization. Included within this component is the clear articulation of the consequences of not achieving full integration and implementation of the new organization's business plan. This plan needs to include both consequences for the organization and consequences individually for the managers attending the session.

This is where managers work with mission, vision, and strategy statements in preparation for passing this information on to their people in a manner that is appropriate to their areas of responsibility. This is best done in small groups of no more than ten people. After each manager has made a first pass at what the statements mean for himself or herself and his or her people and how to best communicate this information, they can share their planning with their small group and discuss it.

This work session is followed by an open forum to raise and discuss any questions, issues, or concerns managers may have with the mission, vision, or strategy, or with any other information they have received, as well as any issues that may have come up in the planning work sessions they have just completed. It is through planning and discussion, both in small groups and in an open forum, that real understanding of the new organization's mission, vision, strategy, and cultural values and what they mean for everyone in the organization is really established.

A very common error in integration work is for this type of information to be sent out in a memo or covered in what is effectively a one-way briefing and left at that. Senior executives are well-advised to remember what it took for them to become comfortable with this same information and to realize that others will need time to digest it. Without spending the time required for full integration, managers will almost certainly default back to the way they have done things before.

Always keep in mind the basic principle of change—*change takes time and mental energy.* Sharing in the process through work sessions with peers is a critical way to help all managers embrace the new ways and learn how to communicate them in a consistent manner across the organization. Without the intense work done in the session, the interaction, and the involvement, it is all too easy for the average manager to file what is said away as "something to do when I have the time" and continue on with business as usual—which cannot be allowed if the cultural integration is to succeed.

VALUES AND PRACTICES

The next component of Step 6 is a review of the new corporate values developed by the executives in their Issues-Based Team-Building Session (Step 5) and seeing how they relate to the new strategy. The values statements highlight what is important to the organization and how the organization intends to operate—its core beliefs or principles. These will be the foundation of the new organization's culture.

Now managers must identify relevant and feasible practices to further define each value and specify day-to-day behaviors that will make the values come alive in the organization. This process takes place in a very dynamic work session that allows every manager to participate fully in the development of a set of practices for each of the values.

The managers, working in groups of ten, are asked to discuss what the new values mean for the management group and what changes in behavior must be made if the values are going to come alive throughout the organization. In effect, each group is asked to do a quick diagnosis, based on their knowledge of various parts of the organization, as to what could prevent the values from becoming real and what behaviors would make the new values truly "the way we do things around here."

It is helpful to have a set of suggested behavioral practices under each of the values as a discussion starter. A sample developed by an actual management team is displayed in Exhibit 7.1.

Exhibit 7.1. Sample Values and Practices

Understanding and Respect

1. Practice active listening.
2. Seek and value each other's input and ask questions.
3. Park my ego.
4. Practice consideration of others (present or not).
5. Comprehend the content, acknowledge the feelings, and respect the views.

Honesty

1. Admit when I'm wrong and acknowledge when I'm uncertain or don't know.
2. Be candid and provide full disclosure.
3. Seek out the truth.

Trustworthiness

1. Be accountable and responsible for my actions and inactions.
2. Make and keep commitments.
3. Confront interpersonal trust issues directly.

One Organization, One Direction

1. Keep our strategic direction at forefront and ensure the goal is clear.
2. Listen, speak up (I don't have a right to remain silent), and support.
3. Share lessons learned and celebrate success.
4. Seek consensus and synergy.
5. Seek simplicity.

The output of this first part of the work session is a set of management practices from each group that they feel are required to support each of the cultural values in the organization at all levels.

GAINING AGREEMENT ON VALUES AND PRACTICES

When the groups have completed this task, the work session then goes on to a series of re-groupings and consolidations to arrive, after a few hours, at an agreed-on set of practices that the management group feels are critical to make the values come alive. The logistics of this consolidation activity depend on the size of the overall group, but the task should be achieved by mid-afternoon of the second day.

It is almost impossible to over-rate the power of this component of the session and the energy and focus it will create among the managers. This is usually the first time that the full management group will have had any open and shared discussion about how they need to manage and behave to fully and successfully make their values a real part of organizational life.

During this work session, it is appropriate and important to allow the group to suggest additional values that they may feel the executive group overlooked and that they feel are vital to the organization. Should they wish to add a value, the managers can make their case to the members of the executive group in attendance, who will decide whether or not it should be included.

This activity of the All-Managers Session closes with a final report from group spokespeople championing each of the values and specifying the practices that have been agreed on. This is followed by an open forum, chaired by the executive team, for open airing of any questions, issues, or concerns that may have come up.

COMMUNICATING THE SESSION RESULTS

The final component of the All-Managers Session includes a reminder from the CEO that the agreed-on management practices will be the way all are expected to manage going forward and that there will be a multi-rater 360-degree feedback system put in place to let each manger know how he or she is doing on demonstrating these practices on the job, as perceived, at the minimum, by their direct reports, peers, and boss. The practices will be the actual survey items to be rated by these various constituencies. (A sample feedback report is presented in Appendix F and also on the accompanying CD-ROM.)

Next is an open group discussion on how the results of the meeting and the process will be communicated back to the rest of the organization.

We recommend that the All-Managers Session be held in a single two-day meeting. Obviously, the number of managers in the organization may preclude a single meeting. We have run these sessions successfully with over one thousand managers attending.

If a series of sessions is required, they should be held over as short a time period as possible. This will require significant coordination and follow-through to assure that the goals are met uniformly across all the sessions. The size of a meeting of this type is effectively limited only by the size of the space available in which to hold the meeting.

TIGER TEAMS

The next step in the alignment and integration process (shown as Step 6a in the nine-step model in Exhibit 6.1) is the investigation and resolution of any infrastructure issues that have surfaced during the CDD or in the Issues-Based Team Building or All-Managers Session by "Tiger Teams." Figure 7.2 shows how tiger teams fit into the larger integration picture.

Tiger teams are groups of three to ten people who take on a particular problem, issue, or possibility that something will affect performance and, with the aid of a manager or consultant acting as coach, drive its resolution in a relatively short time frame—usually two to three weeks.

The team is normally composed of people who are directly involved in the problem, issue, or possibility and who have the capability and knowledge to research and analyze it and make informed recommendations for its resolution. The intent is to demonstrate organizational willingness and ability to take quick and positive action to make things better, thus setting a standard and expectation for the nature of the new organization.

A number of significant infrastructure issues may have been identified at the All-Managers Sessions. These must be resolved before more efficient operations are possible. When this is the case, tiger teams need to be formed to deal with these issues before the organization can proceed with overall alignment. They can also review infrastructure problems and determine how best to resolve them.

Figure 7.2. Tiger Teams

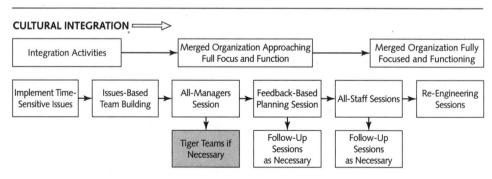

This approach provides lower level management and staff with the opportunity to contribute to the problem-solving process. One of the best approaches tiger teams can employ is a simple three-step method: (1) "as is" analysis; (2) "should be" analysis; and (3) change recommendations and design.

As a CDD will have been completed prior to starting the alignment and integration process, the manager supporting each team can keep the team focused on what has been discovered already, saving considerable time.

The key activities involved at this point are

- *Focused Business Review*—teams of managers conduct a systematic review of a specific sector of the business to identify necessary changes;

- *Active Management Participation*—as part of the design to gain commitment to the proposed solution, managers from the areas to be assessed are assigned to the tiger teams;

- *Skills Transfer*—a series of "just-in-time" workshops to teach analytical tools and consulting skills to the team members;

- *Organizational Simplification and Rationalization*—solutions must be sufficiently simple and rational to be easily communicated to and understood by those who perform the work; and

- *Focus on Solutions That Will Work*—attention of the tiger teams should be focused on practical solutions that can be implemented, that is, that are realistic, achievable, and with a high likelihood of success.

Tiger teams will engage in this special assignment full-time until their task is completed. When the analysis is finished and a recommendation for change is ready to present, the tiger team meets with senior management for review and approval. Ideally, these meetings will be open affairs with quick decisions, much in the manner of the GE "workout method." The idea is to model quick and definitive action for the rest of the organization.

FEEDBACK-BASED MANAGEMENT PLANNING SESSIONS

While the alignment and integration of the management group clearly begins with the All-Managers Session, those sessions are not sufficient to achieve significant modification in day-to-day manager behavior. The next step (the seventh in

Exhibit 6.1) is a series of Feedback-Based Management Planning Sessions to help managers identify the changes and development that they need to model the values and practices on a day-to-day basis. (See Figure 7.3 for its placement in the entire integration process we follow.)

Once the managers have returned to work from the All-Managers Session, they will begin to realize that changing the way they manage is not as easy as they expected. They established a very clear understanding of what was desired in terms of both results and behavior—not insignificant by any means, but still not sufficient for them to create the change.

Two things are now required: (1) time to deal with the necessary changes and (2) initial feedback or baseline data on how each of them is perceived in terms of the organization's new values and practices. The Feedback-Based Management Planning Sessions provide these.

Essentially, these sessions are designed to provide managers with individual feedback on how they are being perceived by employees, supervisors, and peers while they are implementing the new practices. Typically, this feedback is multi-rater or 360-degree feedback on each management practice. The numeric ratings focus on (1) the frequency with which the manager demonstrates the practice and (2) the importance of that practice from the rater's perspective. A sample feedback report is given in Appendix F and on the CD-ROM.

The feedback sessions where the results are shared are quite intense and designed to assure that every aspect of managing and leading in the new organization is dealt with—in an environment of candor, openness, and support. While some behavioral changes may be easy to achieve, many mean changing habits that

Figure 7.3. Feedback-Based Management Planning Sessions

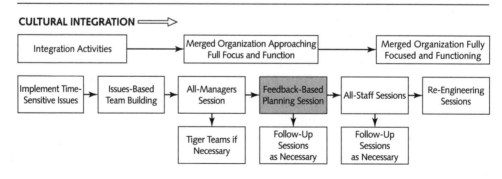

have been years in the making. Changes of this type usually require help from others. To this end, managers work in cross-functional teams, each with its own coach.

These sessions range in time from three to five days, are generally held off-site, and need to be residential or sequestered in nature. To achieve maximum impact, these sessions typically involve morning, afternoon, and evening sessions. We have designed these sessions for a maximum of twenty-eight people per session, preferably no fewer than twenty. Attendees are divided into four teams of five to seven people per team, and each team has its own coach/facilitator for the entire session.

DEVELOPMENTAL STREAMS

Within these sessions we have multiple streams of activity. First, each manager completes (and regularly revisits) a management system analysis of his or her own area of responsibility. This means reviewing the following:

1. The needs, skills, current performance, and track record of each of his or her direct reports;

2. The needs, interests, and track records of peers with whom he or she regularly interacts in accomplishing business responsibilities;

3. The needs, interests, and track record of each of the business units or areas for which he or she is responsible or needs to interact with in the accomplishment of business responsibilities, including the units that provide work as well as the units or customers who receive the work products;

4. The needs, interests, demands, and expectations of his or her own boss; and

5. His or her personal perception of how well he or she is doing in carrying out management and leadership duties.

A sample Manager's Action Planning Guide for this type of analysis can be found in Appendix F and on the CD-ROM that accompanies this book. As in all aspects of this integration and alignment, the particulars for any given activity must be designed to focus attention on the critical aspects of the current business plan. The sample guide is an example of the nature and thoroughness that must be built into this activity.

This analysis must be revisited at least once a day as new information becomes available, such as feedback data, additional knowledge from briefings, skill enhancement sessions, and interactions with the other managers on their teams, as well as the others in their session.

A second critical activity during the session is a methodical review by each manager of his or her own personal drivers, interests, and motivations. Probably many of the things that led to the managers taking management jobs in the company in the first place are changing. How important these changes are for the individual manager can vary quite widely.

It is important that each manager understand what it will mean to be a manager in the new organization and what is now expected of him or her. The definition of success has been altered to some degree for every manager, and so it is beneficial, and only fair, to both the individual manager and to the organization to provide an opportunity for them to reconfirm their desire to function in their jobs, or opt out if it no longer fits.

A third agenda item is the enhancement of necessary skills and knowledge where the CDD or the 360-degree survey has shown a general pattern of deficiency.

Often this deficiency will be in organizational system awareness or a lack of a detailed understanding of the requirements for management and leadership during times of crisis and change. Another typical need is for a better understanding of the operational distinctions between leadership and management and ways in which they carry out these functions. Usually there is also a need during the session to cover rather thoroughly the research on effective leadership and management of significant change in organizations and what this means for how they spend their time in the coming months.

In addition to these broad common areas that usually need enhancement, there are usually a number of specific but just as critical things that vary widely by company. Specific topics such as the competition, enhancing customer service, cross-functional relationships, performance management, and continuous improvement can be covered over the course of the session. Where one company may have a new, heavy emphasis on teamwork and matrix management, another may have an emphasis on more independent operations and local authority. Every company will have its own topics that should be covered, depending on its business needs and requirements.

INDIVIDUAL ACTION PLANS

As each topic is covered, it must be linked to the relevant component of the 360-degree feedback that each manger has received. The manager then uses the specific points when developing his or her individual action plan. In one of the last activities of the session, the managers share their action plans in triads and then with the whole group for a critique and implementation advice.

The final activity of the Feedback-Based Management Planning Session is usually an open forum with the CEO or a member of the executive team. This is designed to be a frank and open exchange of views and information, based on the information and feedback that the managers have received during the session. It is essential that the CEO or the member of the executive team who participates has been through a Feedback-Based Planning Session and has received his or her feedback and developed an individual action plan as well.

FOLLOW-UP SESSIONS

In most instances it is highly recommended that the company hold monthly half-day follow-up sessions for at least six months. Reconnect meetings should be held at thirty, sixty, ninety, and 180 days, at a minimum, with a 360-degree feedback re-survey done in conjunction with the 180-day meeting. (See Figure 7.4 and also Step 7a of the nine-step model.)

Follow-up sessions must be scheduled and run on a team basis. Groups of five to seven managers who were on a team together during the planning sessions thus become ongoing support groups for individual change. By meeting each month

Figure 7.4. Follow-Up Sessions

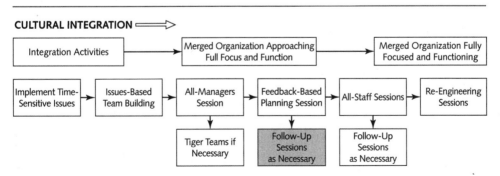

and briefing each other on their individual progress—both successes and problems—in carrying out their action plans, and by amending them as necessary with the support of this group, follow-through is significantly enhanced.

It is extremely difficult for any manager to make commitments to particular actions and then consistently fail when he or she is making those commitments before a group of peers who are making similar commitments. Peer pressure is a far more effective method to get follow-through than are external controls or pressures—and this method more closely reflects the natural establishment and maintenance of desired cultural norms in organizations. We have found that this self-monitoring and correction phenomenon is at the heart of successful organizational cultures.

When the Feedback-Based Management Planning Sessions are well underway within the management group—when at least a third of the managers have completed their initial sessions—the organization is ready to initiate what in many cases may be the final step in the integration and alignment process—the All-Staff Meetings (Step 8 from Exhibit 6.1), which are discussed in the following chapter.

Aligning the Total Organization

THE NEXT STEP IN THE CULTURAL INTEGRATION process is to involve every staff member in order to gain understanding of and commitment to the new organization. This is achieved by involving all the organization's staff in the reasons for the merger or acquisition, the direction of the new organization, and the changes that are required for its success. Every member of the staff must be personally informed and invited to help the new organization succeed. This is accomplished in a series of All-Staff Sessions or "Staff Involvement Days," Step 8 of the model presented in Exhibit 6.1. Its place in the Cultural Assessment and Integration Flowchart is shown in Figure 8.1.

DESIGN AND ACTIVITIES FOR ALL-STAFF SESSIONS

All-Staff sessions are one-day events composed of groups of from twenty to as many as one hundred people at a time. These events are carefully orchestrated sessions where the primary presenters are the organization's executives and senior managers. An outside consultant or facilitator emcees the session and keeps it on

Figure 8.1. All-Staff Sessions

schedule. The participants are divided into discussion groups of no more then ten people at separate tables.

Each small group is facilitated by a manager who has completed the Feedback-Based Planning Session, received the 360-degree feedback, and has developed and is in the process of implementing an individual action plan. It is important that the manager not have any of his or her own direct reports at the table. In this way the manager/facilitator is a representative of management in general, rather than "the boss." This is a critical dynamic in achieving and maintaining the candid and open discussion that is necessary for success. A typical agenda is shown in Exhibit 8.1. A more complete sample with materials is provided in Appendix H and on the CD-ROM.

Exhibit 8.1. Sample Agenda for an All-Staff Session

- Welcome and Preview of the Day
- Introductions
- The Case for Change
- Making a Difference: The Energy Investment Model
- Forces for Change: Organizational and Management Commitments
- Our Vision, Mission, Strategy, Values
- Leadership Mandate: 360-Degree Survey and Management Action
- Making A Difference: Your Personal Challenge
- Making a Difference: Team Ideas for a More Effective Company

---

THE CASE FOR CHANGE

The sessions begin with the "Case for Change," presented by an executive or senior manager, who details the reasons for the merger or acquisition, the direction of the new organization, and the changes that will be required for the new organization to succeed. He or she also is clear about the organizational consequences if those changes do not result in an effective and efficiently implemented commercial reality. When the presentation is complete, each small group goes into a focused discussion of the content of the presentation, facilitated by the manager at that table, followed by a question-and-answer session with the executive or senior manager who made the presentation.

Overview of Organization's Direction

The next activity is a presentation and overview of the direction of the organization—its mission, vision, strategy, and values—with emphasis on a detailed review of the new organization's business strategy. The benefits to all concerned need to be clear and presented with the firm belief that success is clearly within the grasp of the company. The audience again breaks into discussion groups and ends with an open forum discussion with the presenter.

These two activities will often take up most of the morning of this all-day session.

Competitor/Customer Focus

The next activity is optional, and if it occurs it usually involves one of two possible activities—either some form of getting to know the competition or some form of understanding customer perceptions and their implications for how the company will do business in the future. Either of these bolsters the case for the organizational changes that were previously specified.

Values Briefing

The next activity is a briefing on the values and management practices that were decided on by the executives and managers in their sessions. The participants are taken through the values, but the bulk of the time is spent on the new management practices and on a brief review of the nature of the Feedback-Based Management Planning Sessions that were held.

Management Action Plans

The focus then turns back to the individual tables, where the manager at each table walks the group through his or her own personal feedback report and then briefly goes into his or her own personal action plan. This activity has a number of purposes:

1. It gives the staff a chance to see how the feedback they gave in the 360-degree survey is being utilized by the managers. (Remember, by this time most of the people attending will have been asked to fill out feedback forms on their own managers.)

2. The briefing by the manager who is facilitating the group demonstrates the seriousness with which the suggested changes are being taken by the management group as a whole.

3. The point is made that each person's own manager has, or soon will have, an action plan to review with his or her staff. The attendees are encouraged to ask their own managers to share their action plans, if the managers have not done this already.

4. It serves as a demonstration that management is already in the process of creating changes, both organizationally and personally. This is a critical step in most organizations, before asking for the collective input and/or participation of all staff in the change efforts.

Performance Improvement Suggestions

The last activity in the All-Staff Sessions is designed to engage each participant personally. While there are potentially a number of forms this activity may take, two are the most common, in our experience.

The first possibility is a quick work session to develop one or more performance improvement suggestions that the small group feels would make a real difference in overall company results. When this form is utilized, it is imperative that a system be set up prior to the start of the session to review and respond to every suggestion within a few weeks, if not within a few days. Rapid follow-up is critical if staff input is asked for at this point. Lack of rapid and responsive follow-up will destroy staff commitment, when enhanced commitment was the objective.

This does not mean accepting all suggestions or even necessarily implementing suggestions immediately. It does mean responding in a very short time frame to say what is or is not going to happen as a result of the suggestion, and why. For things that cannot be decided or implemented quickly, a date by when the decision will be made or the suggestion implemented should be given.

The second common approach used for this step is a small group discussion on what changes people feel they can make personally that would help in the overall company change. During this discussion, people personally analyze and commit, producing personal action plans that are shared with the rest of the small group.

Either way, this final phase is a clear invitation to the staff to join in and participate in the change effort.

For many organizations, this may be the last step in the alignment and integration of the new organization. At the conclusion of these sessions, the major activities of the integration and required organizational change should be well underway.

WORK-PROCESS RE-ENGINEERING SESSIONS

When the changes being made are quite substantial, there may be the need for one last major event or series of smaller events to successfully integrate the two organizations. Particularly in regard to infrastructure issues, there may be a need for a more concentrated attack through a re-engineering effort that includes staff of all levels (Step 9 in the nine-step model shown in Exhibit 6.1). See the last box on the flowchart in Figure 8.2.

Figure 8.2. Organizational Re-Engineering Sessions

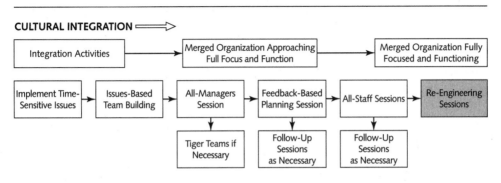

This re-engineering can take either or both of two primary forms. The first and most common is expanded use of "tiger teams" (see the previous chapter) to take on analysis and recommend change.

Another more radical but very effective and fast approach is a large group re-engineering session. This approach is much more effective in dealing with infrastructure issues that cross department boundaries or work units across the organization than are smaller tiger teams or action learning teams.

With this approach, a representative sample of all organizational departments or units, and staff and management levels within those units as well as senior managers responsible for those units, go off-site for up to a week to collectively re-engineer the targeted infrastructure issues. The advantage of this approach is that in one room (often a large ballroom) all the elements of the organizational system involved in the needed changes are present, so the re-engineering process can occur in a rapid and efficient manner. Suggested solutions can be reviewed for impact by all affected parties very quickly, and the re-engineering solution can be finalized by the people present. As all functions and all levels of the organization are represented, a complete review, final decisions, and implementation plans can be made on the spot.

An example of the power of this approach is a session that we facilitated in the U.K. Roughly seven hundred people representing all aspects and levels of a 2,500-person organization were gathered in a very large ballroom for five days and reviewed and re-engineered the processes of the entire organization. Over six hundred processes were reviewed; 40 percent were modified, 12 percent were eliminated, and eleven new processes were implemented. This activity resulted in significant productivity improvements.

While this may seem like an incredible commitment of resources away from the daily tasks of the organization, the overall results that are achieved quickly more than justifies the investment.

Cultural Integration Success Measures

THE SUCCESS OF MERGERS AND ACQUISITIONS can be measured in various ways as components of an "M&A Report Card." Some samples of ways to measure post-merger or integration success, either financially or culturally, are given below.

FINANCIAL SUCCESS MEASURES

The data on the following measures are routinely collected by the finance, legal, and HR departments. The information can be used to monitor and assess organizational performance subsequent to a merger or acquisition.

- Increase or decrease in share price;
- Increase or decrease in revenue;
- Increase or decrease in operating profit;
- Increase or decrease in profitability;
- Payback of capital costs;
- Recovery of any premiums paid;
- Increase or decrease in productivity levels;

- Increase or decrease in market share;
- Loss of key executives; and
- Loss of key staff.

The data on all these measures are routinely collected by the Finance, Legal, and HR Departments and can be used to monitor and access organizational performance subsequent to a merger or acquisition.

CULTURAL INTEGRATION SUCCESS MEASURES

The following measures can be used to determine the progress and status of the cultural integration of two companies after a merger.

1. *Web-Based Staff Opinion/Attitude Survey*—targeted or all-staff sampling at intervals to quantify the staff's perceptions of and satisfaction with the integration activities to date.

2. *Web-Based CDD Re-Survey*—assuming an initial CDD survey was conducted in conjunction with cultural due diligence, targeted samples or the total staff can be re-surveyed at about the mid-point of the integration effort and the results compared to those of the initial survey.

3. *Web-Based 360-Degree Leadership and Management Survey*—assuming an initial 360-degree survey was conducted of all leaders and managers in the organization on the behavioral leadership practices that support each of the organization's core values, follow-up surveys provide individual and collective data on how well the core values and practices are being modeled.

4. *Monitoring of Customer Service Levels and Customer Satisfaction*—assuming such measures currently exist, they can be monitored for variation from the norm. Effective cultural integration will be reflected in initial maintenance of current levels, with a trend upward in both measures as the integration proceeds.

5. *Focus and Monitoring of Current Organizational Measures*—specific focus on and monitoring of current measures of productivity.

6. *"Listening Posts" and Focus Groups*—people within various business units and functions can be assigned "listening post" duty to informally and

periodically gather small groups of staff and ask about their satisfaction with the cultural integration, check for unresolved issues, and ask for suggestions for improvement. This activity can be formalized as periodic focus groups with business units and functions.

7. *Customer Interviews/Focus Groups/Surveys*—assuming full communication to customers about the rationale for the merger and the expected benefits, interviews and focus groups or surveys can be conducted with key customers to assess the customers' perspectives on the merger and how it is playing out in the marketplace.

Staff retention, tardiness, absenteeism, performance to budget, and so on can also provide indicators about the status of the cultural integration. Operational measures of factory through-put, in-process inspection, out-of-box failures, and so on can also be used.

Other measures of cultural integration can be specifically designed and developed as the project parameters become known.

Summary and Conclusion

A CHIEVING POST-MERGER SUCCESS is possible, despite the dismal track record of M&A deals over the last twenty years. It requires a radical change in the prevailing wisdom, which ignores Cultural Due Diligence as a component of traditional due diligence and holds that the cultural impact of the integration has to be survived, rather than proactively managed. A body of knowledge and exemplary examples exist of Cultural Due Diligence and Cultural Alignment and Integration that can help in the successful creation of a strong and dynamic new organization.

An organization's stakeholders—its shareholders, staff, management, customers, suppliers, and residents of the communities in which it does business—should ask tougher questions in advance of any planned merger and acquisition and insist on doing cultural assessment and Cultural Due Diligence before the deal is made, then Cultural Alignment and Integration Planning to guide the development of the new organization.

Members of Boards of Directors, CEOs, and senior executives should keep in mind the growing stakeholder concern with merger and acquisition activity and remember that they are being held increasingly accountable, not just for doing the deal, but for the *success* of the deal as well. They too should insist on Cultural Due

Diligence as part of the initial assessment and Cultural Alignment and Integration Planning as a matter of course in any planned merger or acquisition.

The current track record of M&A failures can and should be reversed, with 77 percent succeeding rather than 77 percent failing. Cultural Due Diligence, together with systemic, data-based integration planning, can help make the difference in reversing the current trend, to the benefit of all organizational stakeholders.

Appendices

The British Airways Transformation

A Systemic Approach

BACKGROUND

The transformation of British Airways (BA) from one of the least favored, most under-performing and unprofitable international carriers in the world in the late 1970s and early 1980s into the world's most profitable airline and one of the most admired airlines by 1996 was, indeed, remarkable. This turnaround has been chronicled over the last twenty years in management literature and the business press as solely or predominantly attributable to a pervasive culture change effort within the airline. In truth, the culture change efforts were a strong driver of the transformation and perhaps the most visible to the public, but certainly not the only driving force.

In fact, careful examination of the history of the transformation (in which we played a part) shows that British Airways, under the bold leadership of Colin Marshall (now Lord Marshall of Knightsbridge) from 1983 to 1995, took a *systemic approach* to transforming its worldwide operations, including downsizing, aircraft fleet replacement, improved infrastructure (for example, computer reservations systems, hub-and-spoke operations, IT decentralization, competitive pricing, and improved terminal facilities, including the opening of Terminal 4 at Heathrow), the innovative branding of the airline's classes of service, and devolution of decision-making authority to line managers. The performance management system and management bonuses were restructured, with 20 percent of salary available calculated fifty-fifty on achieving measurable objectives and on demonstrating desired values and management practices.

In addition, BA engaged in a series of alliances, mergers, and acquisitions, perhaps the most notable being the acquisition of British Caledonian, to strengthen their dominant position at London's Heathrow Airport prior to privatization in 1987.

It was a complex and comprehensive process that lasted for roughly twelve years and involved a number of key initiatives, including but not limited to the much-vaunted culture change initiatives. If any of these key initiatives had been left out, the transformation may well not have succeeded. It was clear to Marshall and his team from the beginning that neither culture change not structural change alone could transform the airline.

THE NEED

When Marshall arrived at BA in 1983, he found an airline that was losing something on the order of £140 million per year—or £200 per minute, 24 hours a day seven days a week. "BA" as the saying went at the time, stood for "Bloody Awful." A 1980 survey by the International Airline Passenger Association placed BA at the top of a list of airlines to be avoided at all costs. The basic attitude of the airline's staff was reflected in the words of a senior manager in 1984 when he said, "We could run a damn fine airline if it wasn't for all those bloody passengers." Further, Prime Minister Margaret Thatcher wanted the airline privatized within five years as part of her government's privatization movement.

THE RESPONSE

Perhaps the most fundamental decisions that Marshall made over the transformation was that British Airways was no longer in the transportation business, but rather in the customer service business, which served to refocus the company's strategy. While many structural changes were in order, it was clear to Marshall that the old quasi-governmental/military culture would not support this shift in focus and strategy and that it would have to be changed. The transformation would require the airline's approximately 50,000 staff to think differently about British Airways, their jobs, and especially about their day-to-day behavior. This was the impetus for the culture change initiatives.

One of the first actions in the transformation did not, however, have to do with the organization's culture and had begun before Marshall arrived. It was a radical downsizing of the airline's bloated staff numbers by 40 percent by the end of 1983. Marshall accelerated this process and included senior management, terminating approximately 150 senior managers in what became known as "the night of the long knives." In addition to significant savings in cost and reduced inefficiency, it certainly got the attention of managers and staff remaining with the airline.

The British Airways culture change effort consisted of a number of initiatives undertaken to transform the organization into a customer-focused, cost-conscious, and profitable airline. An important component of the culture change initiatives was Marshall's "lead from the front" style. He seemed to be everywhere and to never forget the name of a staff member. When he flew, he arrived early and talked with the ground staff, flight crew, and cabin crew. He was known to downgrade himself from first class to business or coach class or off-load himself from the flight based on customer demand. He attended nearly every Managing People First session for a Friday afternoon no-holds-barred question-and-answer session with the participants, and on the rare occasion that he could not attend, he had the participants meet with him in the Board Room at BA's Speedbird House headquarters within days after the course ended. He was even known to pitch in with meal service—and the staff loved him.

The major culture change initiatives and programs from 1983 to 1995 included the following:

- *Putting People First* (1983–1984)—Often described incorrectly as the only culture change initiative, this one-day program was attended by all staff worldwide to achieve focus on becoming a customer service company. Colin Marshall personally attended 95 percent of these programs, describing his vision for BA and engaging in open discussion with participants.

- *A Day in the Life* (1984)—A one-day program attended by all staff worldwide to familiarize them with other areas of the airline, what it was like to work there, and the criticality of all in the organization being sensitive to their impact on others in the company as well as on the customers.

- *Terminal Supervisor Development Program* (1984–1985)—A thirteen-day residence program for all supervisors in the BA terminals. With a new focus on customer service, there were implications for the focus and required skill set of all front-line supervisors in customer service areas. All terminal supervisors went through this program, which covered the new focus and required skills for the redefined terminal jobs. After this program, all those who wished to continue as supervisors in the terminals went through an assessment center as part of reapplying for their jobs.

- *Managing People First* (1984–1990)—A five-and-a-half-day residence program for all managers in the company worldwide, up through the executive levels. This program provided crystal-clear clarity on the new strategy and the implications for management. It included 360-degree feedback for all managers on the new values management practices that were expected going forward. Managers revisited each aspect of their jobs and reformulated how they would go about their jobs in this new environment.

- *Cabin Crew Fleet Director Programs* (1985–1986)—To support the change in the way Cabin Crew were rostered into teams that worked the same flights and shift patterns, a new Fleet Director position was created to provide leadership, support, and management on the ground and in the air. This program equipped the newly appointed Fleet Directors with the required skills to do the job.

- *Leading the Service Business* (1986)—A five-day residence program for the top 150 senior managers, focusing on the leadership requirements and unique management aspects of being at the top of an organization focused on service. This program also covered the leadership requirements of an organization undergoing transformation, and included customized 360-degree feedback for all attending.

- *Performance Appraisal* (1985)—With a new strategy, newly defined jobs, and newly defined management practices, the importance of the performance appraisal system in keeping the focus and demeanor of all staff and management in alignment became critical, and a new system was devised and implemented with management training sessions. Fifty percent of the management bonus was tied directly to demonstrating the new organizational values and practices on the job.

- *IT Reorganization* (1984–1985)—In line with the new strategy, the entire IT organization needed to be completely reorganized and decentralized, with many of the measures of success radically redefined and all staff refocused in terms of purpose. A large-scale change management exercise was undertaken to accomplish this changeover within thirty days.

In 1995, Colin Marshall resigned as CEO of British Airways and become Chairman of the Board, replacing the irascible Lord King. Robert Ayling was promoted to the CEO job. Under Ayling, the culture change initiatives continued, including:

- *Customer Service Leadership Programs* (1988–1989)—One particularly important piece of new strategy was "Brands, Branding, and Brands Camp," the introduction of the innovative concept of branding the airline's four classes of service, based on extensive marketing research. This necessitated a series of five-day programs that were run in Europe, North America, South America, the Middle East, Africa, and Asia for all ground management staff on delivering on brand promise or value proposition to the customer.

- *Winning for Customers* (1990)—A one-day all-staff program to reemphasize the importance of customer focus and customer service. It made extensive use of computer-based simulations of various customer scenarios that involved staff teams in their resolution.

- *Managing Winners* (1992–1993)—A three-day residence program toward the end of the transformation period was attended by all managers and supervisors worldwide. It covered the needs for enhanced quality, cross-system cooperation, and personal development if the improvement patterns and successes were to continue and expand.

- *Leadership 2000* (1998–1999)—A follow-up to the benchmark Managing People First leadership program, which ran from 1984–1990, this program utilized a battery of individual psychometric instruments and an Outward Bound-type component in addition to its strategic and organizational focus. It addressed the current and anticipated leadership needs of the airline at the start of the new millennium.

THE RESULTS

Significant changes in results in terms of cost reduction, revenue generation, customer satisfaction and preference, and staff morale were perceptible within the first two years of the effort. By the end of 1996, in a dramatic reversal of fortune, British Airways was the most profitable major carrier in the world, was the most favored carrier for international travel by business travelers, and was voted the company that most college graduates would like to work for. By 2000, it was the second most-admired company in Europe. Further, the 1987 privatization had been successfully completed and UK shares were trading briskly on the world's stock exchanges.

Again, prevailing wisdom notwithstanding, these results cannot be attributed solely to the significant culture change program that Marshall led, but rather to an integrated organizational system approach that saw many structural changes implemented over 1983–1996 as well. Further, the success of a culture change effort cannot be attributed to a single program, but rather to a carefully planned and implemented sequence of culture change initiatives.

EPILOGUE

It is no secret that British Airways has fallen far from the grace that it had achieved by 1996, and that it currently languishes well down in the league tables of profitable and preferred carriers. Many factors were involved in BA's decline, including the emergence of low-cost airlines like Ryanair and Easyjet, which could seriously undercut BA's fares; the creation of alliances among competitors like the Star Alliance, which includes BA rivals United and Lufthansa; and pressure on BA's dominance of slots at Heathrow. Under Robert Ayling's leadership, BA set out on a long and distracting and ultimately abandoned attempt to forge its own alliance with American Airlines.

Ayling set in motion a £1 billion internal cost-savings program, most of it to come from reduced labor costs, and embarked on a tiered wage scheme that would see cabin crew flying on the same aircraft and doing the same job receiving significantly different compensation. This prompted threats of a cabin crew strike in 1997; and when negotiations broke down with the Transport and Government Workers Union (TGWU), the union called for a series of 72-hour strikes by cabin crew beginning on July 9, 1997.

BA management reacted very heavy-handedly to the situation, with threats of job loss, suits for damages, and so forth. Union picketers reported being videotaped by BA management. On the first day of the strike, three hundred cabin crew declared themselves officially on strike, but another two thousand called in sick on the day. Some 70 percent of BA flights out of Heathrow were canceled. Management's negotiating position and reaction to the strike seemed to all BA staff a direct contradiction of the caring and supportive culture that had been the basis of BA's success, and Ayling's popularity plummeted. Cost of the strike was estimated at £125 million, staff morale was never recovered, and profits nose-dived 61 percent from 1998 to 1999. BA posted a loss of £244 million, its first loss since privatization nearly a decade before.

Ayling was further embarrassed by having to withdraw the new aircraft tail fin design that he had launched at considerable expense, in part due to the publicly expressed displeasure of Margaret Thatcher and the British public. Robert Ayling resigned on March 10, 2000, leaving the formidable task of recovering the hearts and minds of BA's staff and returning the airline to success and profitability to his successor, Rod Eddington.

Organizational Alignment Model
A Reading

WHAT YOU DO THESE DAYS is perhaps not as important as *how you do it*. In today's business environment, new products, services, and technology provide organizations with a short-lived edge over their competition, at best. Sustained success depends on the way those products and services are delivered. The computer industry offers several examples: companies have plunged, almost overnight, from stunning success to failure or near-failure. Often those companies had competitive, or even superior, products. Their failure typically lay not in lack of attention to products, but in lack of attention to people—to how people were supported and managed and to how products were delivered to customers.

Until recently, the proposition that people are an organization's greatest asset has had little more than lip service in many companies. Factors like globalization, mergers, spreading technology, shorter product lifecycles, an emphasis on quality and customer service, and increasing competition—coupled with the kinds of dramatic reversals in fortune described above—are bringing the realization that lip service isn't enough. One result has been increasing interest in organizational culture and its influence on people and their performance.

ORGANIZATIONAL CULTURE

Culture has been described as "the way we do things around here." Thus, culture is not so much *what* people do—the tasks they perform—as *the manner in which they perform those tasks*. Culture refers primarily to a set of behavior patterns that people tend to bring to any task. Changing culture, then, appears to have the potential for greater long-term, sustained benefits than does changing products, services, or delivery methods.

But we are often told that culture change is very difficult, that people will resist it, and that it can take years—not an encouraging prospect for organizations that are watching their competitors rapidly eat up market share.

Much of the literature on culture has focused on categorizing types of cultures—and may use terms like "myths" and "heroes" to describe key components of the culture. This is interesting and informative—but not always helpful in determining what to do about it. While myths and rituals may be meaningful signals of the nature of a culture, it is useful to remember that culture is *behavior*—it is the way people in the organization tend to behave as they go about their work. Culture change, then, is behavioral change. And the technology of behavioral change is not a new one.

So if culture is behavior, why does it appear to be so much more resistant to change than most other behavior? There are at least two key characteristics of behavior patterns that are part of a group's culture:

- *They are group-wide.* Almost everyone in the group will exhibit the behavior pattern. There will therefore be prevailing norms, expectations, and rewards that support the behavior—and often punishment for behavior that does not fit. This makes it difficult for individuals to change culturally determined behavior unless the behavior of others around them changes at the same time or they are placed in a changed environment that supports the new behavior.

- *They are value-driven.* There is usually an underlying belief or value that is linked to culture-based behavior. People will be reluctant to change behavior that is part of the culture, or will find it difficult, unless they see the new behavior as compatible with key cultural values.

The Organizational Alignment Model in Figure B.1 can be used to examine the relationships among the culture of the organization, its business, and its performance.

The model describes two interdependent paths, providing direction for helping people move from the global statement of an organizational mission and vision to specific organizational results:

- *Strategic:* The left-hand path emphasizes what needs to be done: the broad strategic goals the organization will work toward; the objectives that units and individuals must accomplish to carry out those strategies; and the activities that must be performed to meet goals and objectives.

Figure B.1. Organizational Alignment Model

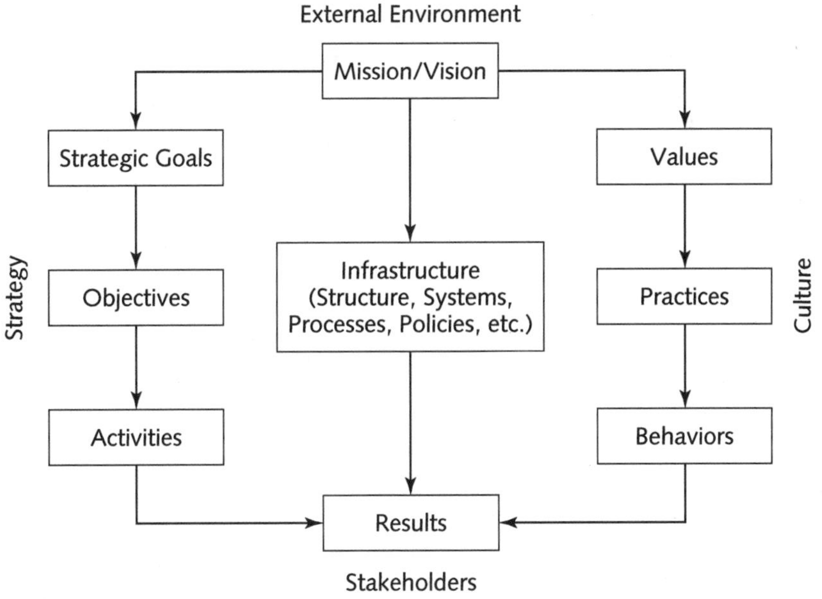

Achieving Post-Merger Success. Copyright © 2004 by John Wiley & Sons, Inc. Reproduced by permission of Pfeiffer, an Imprint of Wiley. www.pfeiffer.com

- *Cultural:* The right-hand path focuses primarily on how it should be done: the values implied by the vision; the practices that reflect those values; and the specific, day-to-day behaviors that will represent the values and practices to others as people go about their work.

ORGANIZATIONAL ALIGNMENT

Any effort to change culture must examine the alignment of *both* paths, providing direction. Organizational alignment consists in compatibility *between* the two paths, and consistency *within* them—the values held in the organization should be compatible with strategic goals; people's day-to-day behaviors should be consistent with the values that they and the organization espouse. For example, a group that strongly values stability should probably not be setting goals around the pork futures market; and the behavior of a group that values responsiveness should not include responding to requests with "Sorry, that's not part of my job."

We should make it clear that we are talking about values around how the organization conducts its business—not people's personal values about home, family, religion, or personal relationships.

Organizations have traditionally emphasized the strategic path. Considerable time and effort often go into defining strategic goals and objectives. Comparatively few organizations have explicitly addressed the cultural path with clearly defined, published statements of values—and fewer have made the effort to examine and support the practices and behaviors that represent those values. *Yet our behavior patterns—the way we do things—are just as important as our activities—what we do—in determining the results we achieve.*

Both strategies and values provide important direction and contribute to organizational success. In recent years, with increasing competition and decreasing differences among many organizations in their technology and products, the "culture values" side of the model—the side most strongly associated with the culture of the organization—has assumed a greater role. When customers perceive less and less difference among companies in the products they provide, they begin to place more and more importance on how those products are delivered and supported.

Below is a brief description of each of the components of the model:

Mission and Vision

Mission and vision represent organizational intent. They serve to provide guidance about organizational purpose, expressed in terms of what the organization is in business to do (mission), with a picture of the expected impact of the organization (vision). For example, here is a mission statement for a hypothetical financial services organization:

> "We provide products and services to business customers that help them make well-informed, timely financial decisions."

Accompanying that mission statement, or as part of it, might be a vision of the organization's impact:

> "We see our customers developing a well-founded confidence in their financial decisions and increasing security about their financial futures."

Those statements provide broad guidance and inspiration to everyone in the organization when making choices about strategies, customers and markets, products, and services, and how to address them.

STRATEGIC GOALS AND VALUES

Strategic Goals and Values provide further direction about where the organization is going, and by what route. They define, in broad terms, how the organization intends to allocate resources to accomplish the mission/vision over time (strategic goals), and how it intends to behave as it does so (values). For example, supporting the mission and vision above might be strategic decisions or goals like these:

- "To provide a full line of financial services focused on small and mid-size organizations."
- "To gain a competitive advantage through top-quality customer service."

These broad goals provide guidance to people in the organization about where they should allocate resources and how they should invest their time and effort. In addition, the organization can make statements about the kinds of values it considers important, such as:

- *Partnering:* "We work in partnership with our customers, freely sharing information, ideas, and plans."

- *Empowerment:* "We encourage people at all levels to take initiative to meet customer needs, and we support them in doing so."

Statements like this provide guidance about customer relations practices and about how people should behave in working with customers.

Mission/vision, value, and strategy statements thus serve to tell people "what we are about" and to guide members of the organization in setting priorities and choosing how to behave.

Objectives and Practices

Objectives and Practices are the institutionalization of strategies and values. They represent decisions about how to implement those strategies and values; the kinds of goals and objectives people set for themselves and the results they expect of their work units; and the typical ways in which they interact with customers and others, both within and outside the organization. For example, managers can support a strategic decision to market to small and mid-size organizations by setting specific sales objectives for those markets or by setting product development objectives around the needs of small and mid-size customers.

People can support a value of partnership by such practices as holding regular joint meetings with clients, or a value of empowerment by ensuring that front-line customer service personnel have adequate resources, support, and authority to take action to meet customer needs.

Activities and Behaviors

Activities and Behaviors are the execution of intent—the ultimate determinants of organizational performance. These represent the next level of specificity—what really happens in an organization on a day-to-day basis: the kinds of activities people choose to spend their time in and the way they behave as they perform those activities. Statements of mission and vision, values and strategies are meaningful only insofar as they are translated into action. For example: A strategic decision to build a competitive edge through customer service becomes reality when people throughout the organization engage in such activities as identifying key customer needs; designing products and services to meet those needs; and delivering and supporting products and services in a way that meets customer needs, preferences, and expectations.

Values of partnership and empowerment become reality when people engage in such behaviors as providing full and accurate information about products and services to customers; making commitments only when they fully intend to meet them; and responding immediately to customer needs, instead of saying things like, "I'll have to check with my supervisor."

Results

Results are the outcomes produced by an organization as a function of the activities and behaviors performed. Results can be measured in a variety of ways: financial indicators, product/service measures, customer satisfaction and retention, sales measures, employee and customer attitude surveys, measures of market share, and so on. The way an organization chooses to measure its performance will determine its ability to "stay on track" and its ability to develop support systems and policies that are in line with values and strategies. For example, an organization that looks at results exclusively in terms of such outcomes as sales volume and profit measures will have a picture of its short-term success, but will lack information that may be critical to its long-term health, such as customer satisfaction and retention measures.

ORGANIZATIONAL INFLUENCES

The paths described above do not, of course, operate in isolation. They influence, and are influenced by, the *external environment* in which the organization operates, the organization's *infrastructure,* and its *stakeholders,* as seen in the model and described below.

External Environment

The External Environment includes factors over which the organization has limited influence, such as the economy, the sociopolitical environment, competition, governmental policies and regulations, and the state of technology. Any or all may influence an organization's choice of strategy or beliefs and values. For example, heavy competition in the large corporate market and expensive technology required to penetrate it may enter into an organization's decision to concentrate on the small and mid-size business market. Increasing recognition of the effects of the organization's actions on the physical environment may result in its placing greater importance on social responsibility as a value.

Stakeholders

Stakeholders are groups that are significantly affected by the organization's performance, such as customers, shareholders, suppliers, or even the general public. These groups have different relationships with, and expectations of, the organization; understanding these expectations is a key factor in organizational decision making. For example, while shareholders and financial analysts may judge an organization heavily in terms of its growth or profits, customers may be making their evaluations on such factors as responsiveness, quality and range of services, or environmental sensitivity. The organization needs to take both sets of expectations into account.

Infrastructure

Organizational support mechanisms, systems, policies, and structures function as "performance levers" that help (or hinder) people in carrying out the activities and behaviors required to implement strategies and values and to produce the desired organizational results. These include such factors as formal and informal reward and recognition systems; information and measurement systems; performance appraisal, compensation and benefits; design of the physical environment; organizational structure and reporting relationships; training and development; job definition and work design; and administrative policies. For example, compensation and reward systems for salespeople that focus exclusively on reaching revenue targets can cause pressure to violate values about treatment of customers, as well as strategic plans for penetrating selected markets. Similarly, centralized control policies designed to bring about consistency can get in the way of responding to customer needs unless those policies are flexible and balanced by reward systems or other factors that support responsiveness to customers.

By dealing with these last three phenomena in a few paragraphs, we don't mean to imply that they are simple or minor issues—but the focus of our model is on organizational alignment and culture. We recognize that stakeholders and environment are major determinants of organizational decision making and that what we've called "support" here summarizes the entire field of performance technology.

Organizational alignment occurs when strategic goals and cultural values are mutually supportive, and when key components of the model are linked and compatible with each other. For example, market strategies should be consistent with organizational values and so perceived by members of the organization; unit objectives should be derived from organizational strategy and supported by management practices; people's day-to-day activities and behaviors should be consistent with mission, strategy, and values; and organizational systems and policies should support those activities and behaviors.

It's unlikely, and even undesirable, that any organization will reach perfection in all these areas. The goal should be to provide enough compatibility and consistency so that people can devote most of their energies toward positive accomplishment of results—with a minimum of their effort directed to overcoming obstacles and a reasonable minority of effort devoted to healthy dissent.

All too often, managers focus almost exclusively on strategic issues in planning, and they then find that results have been achieved at very high cost—or have been blocked entirely by an incompatible culture. Consistent failure to examine values as well as strategies has resulted, for some organizations, in serious discrepancies between organizational strategy and culture. Conversely, many culture change efforts have failed to adequately address the relationship between culture and the multiplicity of factors in the organization that influence it and are influenced by it.

There are those who say that management consultants, trainers, organizational designers, and the ilk have no business messing around with people's values. We don't advocate "messing around" with them—but we do think anyone planning a significant intervention has an obligation to take them into account.

Further, addressing organizational values in the organizational planning process does not mean changing them. Rather, it means clarifying them and understanding their relation to other facets of the model and to current behavior.

Changing values is difficult; they are often developed over a long period of time and drive many behaviors. Changing behaviors is less difficult—particularly if people see the new behavior as compatible with some existing values, as is often the case. This recognition is not automatic, however, and requires particular attention when a set of behaviors has been so strongly linked with a value over time that it has taken on the "status" of a value.

For instance, an organization that has strongly valued quality—and has a history of providing top-of-the-line products at a premium price—may find that, over time, people have come to see "quality" as synonymous with providing products that incorporate the latest technology, the very best materials, and maximum performance capability. If that organization then wants to serve a broader market, it may need to invest extra effort in building a link between the value of quality and a decision to provide products by using a lower level of performance but that nevertheless fully meet or exceed the needs and expectations of customers. Both Volkswagen and Rolls Royce, for example, have reputations for providing quality products—but serve different markets and customer needs.

The resources and effort invested in organizational alignment offer enormous potential payoffs to the organization, its people, and its customers—in profits, job satisfaction, quality of service, and long-term organizational health.

Organizational System Scan Model

An Overview

Purpose: To gather current data on the *"organizational situation,"* as perceived by its functions and people, for use in decision making by top management. The *Organizational System Scan* clarifies organizational intent and direction and captures information about the "real" organization's alignment with that direction—its values and belief system, day-to-day life, and priorities—in short, its culture. It also assesses relevance and helpfulness of organizational systems, policies, and procedures.

Benefits: • Provides the CEO/top management with an efficient and comprehensive diagnostic scan of the organization at all levels;

• Identifies areas of potential greatest leverage for increasing organizational effectiveness as desired;

• Indicates priorities for action to move/transform the organization, which focuses and facilitates planning;

• Provides an assessment of the organization's readiness for change and the adequacy of the organization's leadership and management to effect that change; and, perhaps most significantly

- Enables the alignment of the organization's strategy, culture, and support systems to the business reality confronting it.

An organizational scan can have a primarily *internal, external,* or *combined* focus, depending on specific need. The internal scan looks primarily at the organizational entity as it functions within its business context. The external scan focuses more heavily on constituencies and factors outside the organization that significantly impact upon it—customers, suppliers, alliances, and competitors.

The combined organizational scan is essentially a process of corporate due diligence, focusing primarily on two organizations considering a strategic alliance, marketing partnership, acquisition, or merger. It highlights the cultural factors of both organizations that either support or mitigate against a successful alliance/merger.

A similar process and sequence is employed in all three of the focus options:

Documentation Review:	Examination of all relevant documentation on the organization's conditions, process, and outcomes. Policy and procedures manuals, annual reports, strategic plans, newsletters, and other documents are reviewed.
CEO Interview:	A one-to-one interview to determine the CEO's view of the organization's direction, strategy, culture, health, and needs and to determine the business context in which the organization is operating.
Senior Management Interviews:	One-on-one interviews of members of the top management team—heads of functions, departments, and support units—to gain their perspective on the organizational situation.
Core Samples:	Targeted focus groups representing all levels of the organization, either within functions (vertically) or between functions (horizontally) to develop a profile of the "real" organization and its culture.

Workplace Observation: Informal observations in the various worksite environments, at various times of the work day, to get a feel for the work, the physical environment, climate, and morale.

The data and information collected by means of the organizational scan process are analyzed, consolidated, and reported to the CEO and top management in the form of findings, examples/evidence, and specific recommendations for action. They are arrayed in rank order, from most serious or critical to least serious or critical.

Recommendations take the form of suggested interventions within the organization. The arena of possible interventions is wide, and selection of the appropriate interventions is a key step, as is their implementation sequence. A partial listing of possibilities includes training, cross-functional partnering, process re-engineering, leadership development, executive coaching, information systems modification, employee communication forums, and others. Key to this process is that interventions are based on comprehensive diagnosis, that is, the organizational scan.

ORGANIZATIONAL SCAN DOMAINS

The following organizational domains are examined during the organizational scan, in order to determine their characteristics, interaction, and alignment with the intended direction and strategic goals of the organization.

- External Business Environment
- Mission/Vision
- Strategy/Goals
- Values
- Structure
- Leadership
- Management

- Management Practices
- People
- Climate
- Policies/Procedures
- Systems
- Work Processes
- Objectives
- Measures
- Workplace Environment
- Products/Services
- Organizational Results

These domains are consistent with our Organizational System Scan Model, discussed in Chapter 3 of this book and shown in Figure C.1.

Figure C.1. Organizational System Scan Model

	CONDITIONS	PROCESS	OUTPUTS
EXTERNAL FACTORS	**Marketplace** • World economy • Geopolitical climate • Regulation • Competitors • Technology • Location • Business cycle	**Investment** • Strategic alliances • Partnerships • Mergers and acquisitions • New product development • Privatization • IPOs	**Positioning** • Market share/ dominance • Economies of scale/scope • Reduced vulnerability • Increased revenue • Globalization • New markets
ORGANIZATION	**Direction** • Business situation • Mission/vision • Strategy • Structure • Goals	**Systems** • Planning • Policy/procedure • Support • Information systems • Budgeting • Monitoring	**Results** • Success measures • Profitability • Competitive position • Stakeholder satisfaction
PEOPLE	**Values and Beliefs** • Ideal values • Actual values • Climate • Objectives and demands • Expectations • Politics	**Leadership/Management** • Practices/behaviors • Selection/development • Reward/recognition • Skill/knowledge • Motivation/feedback	**Productivity** • Performance levels • Morale • Empowerment • Loyalty/commitment • Business awareness • Continuous improvement
WORK	**Resources** • Workload • Schedules/cycles • Tools/equipment • Data/information • Physical environment	**Methods** • Work processes • Resource allocation • Process monitoring • In-process correction • SOPs	**Products/Services** • Product/service delivery • Customer satisfaction • Quality • Quantity • Service levels

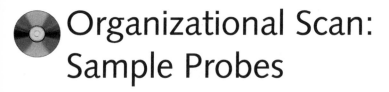

Organizational Scan: Sample Probes

Location: External Conditions—Marketplace

- What world economic conditions are relevant to the organization's performance?

- What factors indicate that a market need/opportunity/demand exists? How has the competition responded?

- Who is the competition? What do they do better? Where is the competition vulnerable?

- How intense is the rivalry among existing competitors? What impact does that have on your business?

- What external rules, regulations, and requirements create or define the market?

- What factors affect the availability of and access to raw materials and component parts?

- Are there governmental or social restrictions on entering or exiting a market?

- What are the economic conditions in each of the countries/regions where the organization operates?

- What language and cultural barriers might have an impact on the organization's products and services?
- What important governmental, social, and political factors present opportunities or threats?
- To what extent has the organization developed and advanced technology? The competition? The industry?

Location: Organizational Conditions—Direction

- What is the organization's mission? Vision? Goals? Values?
- Does the organization have clearly defined strategies for addressing its market?
- Are the strategies communicated throughout the organization?
- Have the organization's strengths, weaknesses, opportunities, and threats been addressed in the strategy?
- Are the missions and goals consistent/aligned across units?
- Are unit goals compatible with others with whom the units must work?
- Are long-term and short-term goals compatible? Is the balance appropriate to the strategy?

Sample Values and Practices

Put Customers First

Service to customers drives our thinking, implementation, and support:

1. Identifies the customer;

2. Demonstrates an understanding of the customer's business;

3. Agrees requirements with the customer aligned to business needs;

4. Manages expectations by promising what we can deliver and always delivering what we promise;

5. Regularly seeks and acts on customer feedback;

6. Jointly manages the impact of actions with the customer; and

7. Represents the customer's needs in everything that we do.

Work as One Team

Actively creating and participating in teams to achieve shared company goals:

1. Utilizes people's strengths and encourages development;

2. Works with others to overcome obstacles;

3. Agrees on clearly defined, measurable objectives;

4. Agrees on clearly defined roles and responsibilities;

5. Shares success;

6. Respects other people's ideas and views; and

7. Encourages and supports team decisions.

Be Open and Involving

Encouraging widespread responsible involvement and open exchange of views with mutual respect and a clear framework for decision making:

1. Provides timely, open, honest, and constructive feedback;

2. Engages the right people in active debate;

3. Treats all information as sharable by default;

4. Actively listens to and respects other people's ideas and views;

5. Encourages constructive challenge; and

6. Discusses and explains the rationale behind decisions.

Move Quickly into Action

Be positioned to assess and reconfirm our priorities and proactively address known problems:

1. Takes and manages measured risk;

2. Empowers and supports people to take responsibility and make decisions;

3. Removes unnecessary complexity from processes/solutions;

4. Positions capability to achieve objectives;

5. Sets and agrees on clear priorities; and

6. Engages the support of others.

Deliver Quality and Innovation

Finding better ways to deliver against expectations and new ways to exploit technology:

1. Delivers fit-for-purpose solutions using agreed-on best practices;
2. Uses measurements and metrics to improve quality and performance;
3. Demonstrates and promotes continuous improvement;
4. Markets and showcases new ideas and technologies;
5. Creates and encourages an environment of innovation and creativity;
6. Evaluates external practices and products against our own and adopts the best; and
7. Constructively challenges the status quo.

Think and Act Like Owners

By identifying the business need in all that we do and taking personal responsibility for the effective use of resources:

1. Considers the real cost, impact, and benefits of actions;
2. Aligns actions with business plans and priorities;
3. Acts as an ambassador for the company;
4. Takes accountability for own actions;
5. Takes action to reduce inefficiencies;
6. Demonstrates leadership and direction; and
7. Takes ownership for self-development.

Sample Manager 360-Degree Feedback Report

For A. Manager in XYZ Corporation

Figure F.1a. Sample Feedback Report

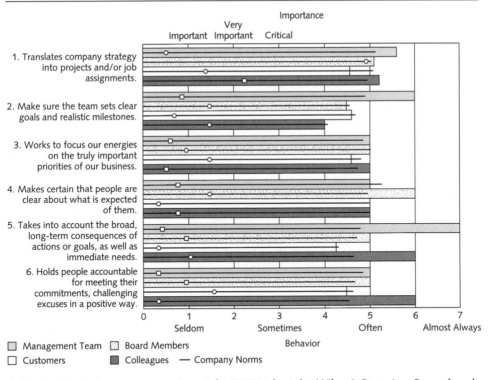

Figure F.1b. Sample Feedback Report

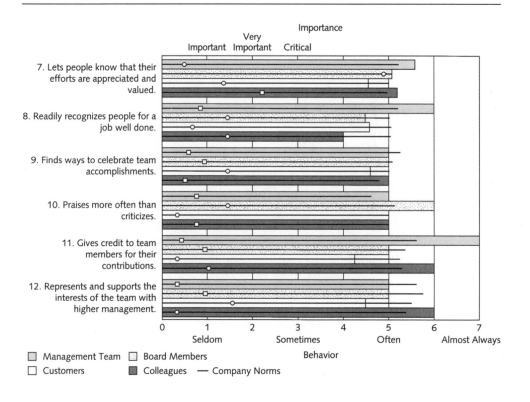

Figure F.1c.   Sample Feedback Report

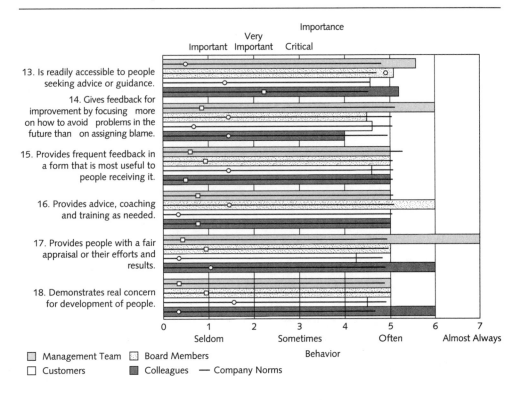

Sample Manager's Action Planning Guide

LEADING PRIDE WORKSHOP*

A Guide to Reflection, Review, Planning, and Implementation of Personal Leadership Development

Your Name:_____

Telephone Number:_____   E-Mail Address:_____

Coach's Name:_____   Workshop Date:_____

Reflecting on Your Behaviour as a Leader and Manager

*The materials in this Appendix were developed in the UK for a UK client and deliberately selected as such for inclusion in the book.

Achieving Post-Merger Success. Copyright © 2004 by John Wiley & Sons, Inc. Reproduced by permission of Pfeiffer, an Imprint of Wiley. www.pfeiffer.com

INTRODUCTION

Increased self-awareness through feedback is a fundamental cornerstone of learning and personal growth. Toward this end, this Guide has been developed to enhance your insight into your management practices and to help you organise and understand the feedback you are about to receive as it relates to you personally.

The Guide will assist you in analysing your feedback and planning steps for future action. You will be asked to answer questions that pertain to the feedback you received and to record your associated thoughts, feelings, and other considerations in the appropriate places. At the end of this process you will be able to make informed judgements concerning those practices and behaviours you should continue to emphasise and those you should change. Working in this Guide may be the single most important activity of your participation in the program.

The feedback given to you is *confidential* and *for your personal use only.* You may at times wish to discuss with other people what you write in your Guide, but that is strictly your choice.

GAINING PERSPECTIVE

Improving your management behaviour is a dynamic, continuous, and, in a very real sense, never-ending process. Ultimately, exceptional management is characterised by continuous striving to create an environment conducive to high-quality performance. The Guide will help you to become this kind of manager by highlighting the changes you and others believe are important for you to make.

THREE THINGS TO KEEP IN MIND

As you work through the Guide, keep in mind three principles that will make the data more meaningful and useful to you:

First, remember that the feedback process is designed to help you better manage your organisation. So whatever your scores are, you will gain the most by exploring how the information can help you solve problems and take advantage of opportunities.

Second, although it is not easy, try to move as quickly as possible beyond any defensive feelings you may experience. If the feedback is similar to what you expected, do not trivialise it. If the feedback is different from what you expected, try to work through it so that you can begin solving the problems that the feedback suggests. One strategy many people have used to reduce their defensiveness is to think about the kinds of defences they usually use and then consciously trying to avoid them. In the margin of this page, jot down some notes to yourself about the ways you may defend against "bad news." This can help you get beyond these defenses quickly.

Third, this report reflects the *collective* view of your behaviour. Some parts of the feedback will confirm your perceptions; other parts may surprise you. While there is a natural tendency to reject information that is less satisfying, doing so can reduce the value of the most relevant data. Therefore, before disregarding any feedback, carefully consider what the information might mean.

PART 1: PUTTING YOUR FEEDBACK INTO CONTEXT

Examining your particular position with regard to your Managerial Situation, Work Situation, and People Situation, as defined below, will help you to analyse the feedback you receive and determine which management behaviours you need to emphasise and apply.

Managerial Situation

Your *managerial situation,* or the degree of authority associated with your position, determines, in part, the way in which you should interpret the feedback you receive. If you are in a "line" function—that is, a manager responsible for an operational group—you have a certain amount of position power that allows you to manage in ways that are less available to people in "staff" functions. If, on the other hand, you are in a staff function, you have very little position power. Any power you do have is primarily a function of your ability to personally influence others. Thus, the way you manage is likely to be quite different.

Considering your type or degree of authority, respond briefly to the following questions.

Questions to Consider: Your Managerial Situation

1. Is the power associated with your position clear-cut; that is, do you and others know quite well the degree of authority you have?

2. To what degree can you individually reward and discipline people in your organisation?

3. Your power is, in part, a function of the combination of your position and your individual expertise. Which source of power is the stronger one for you?

4. Based on your answers to the three questions above, what are implications for you in terms of management behaviours you need to emphasise?

Work Situation

The management behaviours that you utilise are also determined by the nature of your *work situation,* that is, the degree of clarity and structure associated with your job and responsibility. The greater the clarity and structure in your work, the better you will know which management behaviours work effectively.

Taking your work situation into account, respond briefly to the following questions.

Questions to Consider: Your Work Situation

1. How clearly defined are the objectives for your area of responsibility?

2. Is there a "blueprint" for your area of responsibility; that is, are processes and procedures clearly and specifically defined for you or do you have to define them?

3. To what extent are you able to know when your tasks or milestones have been successfully completed?

4. Based on your answers to the three questions above, what are the implications for you in terms of which *practices* you need to emphasise?

People Situation

The characteristics of the people you manage, specifically the cultural, educational, and technical background of your work group members, as well as their level of responsibility, diversity, and degree of team interaction, necessitate that certain management behaviours be emphasised.

With the kinds of people you manage in mind, please respond briefly to the following questions.

Questions to Consider: Your People Situation

1. To what degree do your people have the technical knowledge and skills needed for their jobs? How do you compare this level of technical expertise with your own?

2. What differences exist among the individuals in your group in terms of age, education, experience, and cultural background? How do these differences affect your approach to managing them?

3. How ready is each individual to handle more responsibility and therefore free up some of your time?

4. How important is teamwork in accomplishing your work group's objectives? Is cooperation critical to success? How does this impact your managerial approach?

5. Where is each individual in terms of his or her career? To what extent is each of them actively seeking developmental opportunities? What opportunities for growth and development are there within your group?

PART 2: REVIEWING YOUR FEEDBACK

This section of the Guide will help you plan for changes you would like to make in the way you manage people.

By working through this section, you will

- Decide which aspects of your management behaviour should be targeted for change;
- Develop strategies to capitalise on your managerial strengths and improve the way you manage people;
- Make plans for integrating desired changes into your everyday behaviour; and
- Identify specific developmental needs and plans for fulfilling them.

Completing this section of your Guide is very important in that it translates the learning you have gained from the feedback sessions into meaningful plans for positive change. Therefore, please devote ample time to completing the worksheets contained in this section. Since it is likely that you will return to this report at some point in the future, the more candid and comprehensive your responses to questions, the better able you will be to accurately remember what you planned to change as a result of your feedback—and why you planned to change it.

Throughout the course of this program, you have received a great deal of feedback on the way you manage others. Much of this feedback is a direct reflection of how you and others see your behaviour—the specific attributes you possess, the behaviours that you tend to give more or less attention to, as well as aspects of your personality that affect your management style. To help you sort through your feedback and develop specific strategies for improving the effectiveness of your work group, there are four types of worksheets contained in this section:

- Summarising Data
- Selecting Target Areas
- Planning Your Strategy
- Identifying Developmental Needs

Summarising Data

To begin the process of planning for change, you need to look for patterns in the feedback you have received throughout the program. To help you identify patterns in your feedback, two Summarising Data worksheets are provided, one for identifying areas on which to capitalise and another for identifying areas that need improvement. Use these worksheets in any way that is helpful to you. You can check the competencies that apply, record actual practice scores, or list the actual practices that are most outstanding.

The criteria used to synthesise information in this worksheet relate mostly to *others'* rating. While your own ratings are useful in terms of clarifying where *you* see your areas of emphasis, others' ratings are of primary importance when you are choosing areas on which to focus your change efforts. Even if others' perceptions differ from yours, their ratings reflect *their* reality. In order to help them to be more effective, it is necessary to see things from their perspective.

Selecting Target Areas

Using the information contained in the Summarising Data worksheets, you will be asked to select what you believe are the target areas on which you should concentrate to improve your effectiveness as a manager and to improve the effectiveness of your group. You may choose to focus on changing your behaviour as it relates to one particular piece of your feedback, or you may elect to modify your general management style based on an overall pattern you perceive in your data. The choice of *what* to change and *how* to change it is entirely yours—what is important is that you select target areas that you are *motivated* to pursue.

Planning Your Strategy

To plan for change in each of your target areas, complete the Planning Your Strategy worksheets. These will help make your plans specific and realistic—two criteria necessary for successful change. Thorough completion of these worksheets will help you to take important learnings from this program "back home" and integrate the strategy you develop into your everyday managerial behaviour.

Identifying Developmental Needs

Of longer-term value, even greater than implementing the strategy and actions planned in the previous step, is identifying your continuing developmental needs and making plans for their fulfilment. These worksheets will help you focus on and identify those needs and begin taking action on them.

SUMMARISING DATA: AREAS ON WHICH TO CAPITALISE

When given feedback, managers tend to focus first, if not exclusively, on the negative. Particularly when planning for the future, people are inclined to concentrate on behaviours they need to *change*. But there is much to be gained from examining the areas that you currently emphasise. Understanding where and when you focus and *expanding* the impact of your abilities can help you to be a more effective manager.

To begin the process of planning for the future, complete the following worksheet. Fill out the first column by using the following three criteria as you consider each core competency.

High Ratings from Others

These are practices that others identify as very characteristic of you (ratings above 1.0 or higher). This feedback shows where people see your emphasis and should lead you to consider ways in which you may capitalise on these apparent abilities. This does not necessarily mean, however, that you should *de-emphasise* those practices that received ratings of high emphasis. A high emphasis, together with a high importance rating, may mean you need to keep it up. A lower importance may mean you can reduce time spent on that practice.

Congruence Among Self and Others

Research shows that congruence (a difference of less than .5 points) between your rating of an item and the ratings given by others suggests self-awareness. A manager who is self-aware can identify areas on which to capitalise and can utilise this knowledge to become more successful.

Other Ratings That Are at Significant Variance

It can be very worthwhile to consider why it is that you come across so differently to different people and what that might say about behaviours you may need to change. If ratings given to you by others vary significantly from group to group, this indicates that you exhibit a practice significantly more with some groups than you do with others.

SUMMARISING DATA: AREAS NEEDING IMPROVEMENT

In any feedback profile there is room for improvement. Even in a profile that contains consistently similar ratings, there are ratings that are *lower* than others and ratings that the recipient expected would be *higher*. As was stated earlier, while it is natural to be somewhat anxious when reviewing your feedback, lower or unexpected ratings should not be viewed negatively but as *areas needing improvement*. The foundation of positive change is awareness of what needs to change. Your feedback profile is intended to facilitate this awareness so that you can focus your attention and effectively target your improvement efforts.

To begin the process of planning for the future, complete Worksheet B. Use the following three criteria to consider each core competency.

Worksheet A: Areas on Which to Capitalize

Core Competencies	1 High Numbers	2 Congruence	3 Variance	Comments
Dependability				
Honesty and Openness				
Loyalty				
Ownership				
Urgency				
Risk				
Motivation				
High Expectations				
Recognition				

Achieving Post-Merger Success. Copyright © 2004 by John Wiley & Sons, Inc. Reproduced by permission of Pfeiffer, an Imprint of Wiley. www.pfeiffer.com

Worksheet B: Areas in Need of Improvement

Core Competencies	1 Low Numbers	2 Discrepancies	3 Variance	Comments
Dependability				
Honesty and Openness				
Loyalty				
Ownership				
Urgency				
Risk				
Motivation				
High Expectations				
Recognition				

Achieving Post-Merger Success. Copyright © 2004 by John Wiley & Sons, Inc. Reproduced by permission of Pfeiffer, an Imprint of Wiley. www.pfeiffer.com

Lower Ratings from Others

These are practices that others identify as exhibited to a lesser extent. This information highlights obvious areas for potential improvement, particularly where the importance rating is high. If the importance score is low, as well as the execution score being low, the rating may be appropriately low, requiring no changes.

Discrepancies in Self Versus Other Ratings

A significant discrepancy between your rating of an item and that given by others suggests that you and they have different views regarding this practice.

Other Ratings That Are Significantly Different

If ratings given to you by others vary significantly from group to group, this indicates that, according to some groups, you exhibit this practice significantly *less* with them than you do with others. This information is important in that it provides you with another frame of reference when determining where to focus your change efforts.

PART 3: SELECTING TARGET AREAS AND PLANNING YOUR STRATEGY

Worksheets A and B should begin to give you a sense of the pattern of your management style—where you are giving emphasis and where you need to focus more of your attention, as well as your developmental needs. You may have been aware of some of these issues before asking for feedback; on the other hand, some of these issues may be new to you. In any case, it is now time to move from thinking about your feedback to *doing* something about it.

Use Worksheet C, Selecting Your Target Areas, to capture issues on which you plan to take immediate action. Begin by considering your current areas of emphasis and how you might like to reinforce these; then move on to areas to which you are giving less emphasis. You may find that what you would like to change in one target area has positive implications for other target areas. This can help you to maximise the benefits of your efforts.

Worksheet C: Selecting Your Target Areas

Reinforcement Area 1

_____

_____

_____

_____

_____

Reinforcement Area 2

_____

_____

_____

_____

_____

Improvement Area 1

_____

_____

_____

_____

_____

Improvement Area 2

_____

_____

_____

_____

_____

Before selecting your target areas, you may find it useful to refer to the questions you answered regarding your personal situation earlier in this Guide. Changes you plan to make in the way you manage others should be well grounded in the realities you face back home.

Once you have selected your target areas, take them one at a time and complete Worksheet D, Planning Your Strategy.

Worksheet D: Planning Your Strategy

Reinforcement Area 1

Describe your current situation:

Why do you think you received the ratings that relate to this reinforcement area?

What actions might you take to capitalise on these areas of emphasis, that is, what actions could you initiate or what new activities could you engage in that might take advantage of your focus in this area?

When should these actions be taken (specific dates and time frames)?

(Continued)

Worksheet D: Planning Your Strategy (Continued)

Reinforcement Area 1

Who else needs to be involved in or apprised of your actions?

What are the implications or potential consequences of your actions?

What are the potential obstacles to your taking action?

How and when will you measure progress?

What will be the indicators of success/failure?

Worksheet D: (Continued)

Reinforcement Area 2

Describe your current situation:

Why do you think you received the ratings that relate to this reinforcement area?

Describe your ideal situation:

If the actions you decide to take to improve this area are successful, what will your situation look like?

When should these actions be taken (specific dates and time frames)?

(Continued)

Reinforcement Area 2

Who else needs to be involved in or apprised of your actions?

What are the implications or potential consequences of your actions?

What are the potential obstacles to your taking action?

How and when will you measure progress?

What will be the indicators of success/failure?

Worksheet D: (Continued)

Improvement Area 1

Describe your current situation:

Why do you think you received the ratings that relate to this improvement area?

Describe your ideal situation:

If the actions you decide to take to improve this area are successful, what will your situation look like?

When should these actions be taken (specific dates and time frames)?

(Continued)

Achieving Post-Merger Success. Copyright © 2004 by John Wiley & Sons, Inc. Reproduced by permission of Pfeiffer, an Imprint of Wiley. www.pfeiffer.com

Worksheet D: Planning Your Strategy (Continued)

Improvement Area 1

Who else needs to be involved in or apprised of your actions?

What are the implications or potential consequences of your actions?

What are the potential obstacles to your taking action?

How and when will you measure progress?

What will be the indicators of success/failure?

Achieving Post-Merger Success. Copyright © 2004 by John Wiley & Sons, Inc. Reproduced by permission of Pfeiffer, an Imprint of Wiley. www.pfeiffer.com

Worksheet D: (Continued)

Improvement Area 2

Describe your current situation:

Why do you think you received the ratings that relate to this improvement area?

Describe your ideal situation:

If the actions you decide to take to improve this area are successful, what will your situation look like?

When should these actions be taken (specific dates and time frames)?

(Continued)

Improvement Area 2

Who else needs to be involved in or apprised of your actions?

What are the implications or potential consequences of your actions?

What are the potential obstacles to your taking action?

How and when will you measure progress?

What will be the indicators of success/failure?

DEVELOPMENTAL NEEDS

Given the feedback you have received, and the management and leadership concepts that have been reviewed, what are the areas of longer-term developmental need that require your personal focus and effort over the next months and years? Fill out Worksheet E as a beginning place for your personal development.

Worksheet E: Developmental Needs

DEVELOPMENTAL NEED	EVIDENCE/ IMPORTANCE	DEVELOPMENTAL ACTIVITY (Training, Reading, University Program, Developmental Assignment, Experience, Mentoring)

Achieving Post-Merger Success. Copyright © 2004 by John Wiley & Sons, Inc. Reproduced by permission of Pfeiffer, an Imprint of Wiley. www.pfeiffer.com

Staff Involvement Day
Sample Agenda and Materials

PROGRAMME GOALS*

At the end of the day, participants in the programme will

- Understand the Case for Change and the business and economic reasons driving recent and planned change;
- Understand the impact of their attitude about the company and the energy that they put into the job on the company's success;
- Be clear on the specific organisational and management commitments in progress or planned to address key business issues;
- Understand what the company's vision, mission, strategy, and values mean for their jobs;
- Understand the company's values and practices, and the 360-degree leadership survey feedback reports to managers;
- Individually identify and take actions that will directly contribute to the vision, mission, strategy, and values; and

*The materials in this Appendix were developed in the UK for a UK client and deliberately selected as such for inclusion in the book.

- Collectively recommend actions and initiatives for consideration by the executive board and senior management that will help the company succeed.

STAFF INVOLVEMENT DAY AGENDA

- Welcome and Preview of the Day
- Introductions
- The Case for Change
- Question-and-Answer Session
- Forces for Change: Organisational and Management Commitments
- Lunch
- The Company's Vision, Mission, Strategy, Values
- Leadership Mandate for 360-Degree Survey and Management Action
- Making a Difference: Your Personal Challenge
- Making a Difference: Team Ideas to Make the Company Better
- Closing Comments

STAFF INVOLVEMENT DAY GROUND RULES

It is helpful to have established and mutually understood "ground rules" regarding the individual and group responsibilities of all participants.

Proposed ground rules for today include:

- *Timekeeping*—Start and complete all activities on time.
- *Mutual Respect*—Treat all participants, presenters, and team coaches with respect.
- *Honesty and Openness*—Raise any issue or concern and get a fair hearing.
- *Confidentiality*—Maintain confidentiality of information if requested.
- *Program Environment*—Work together to help create an adult, participative, enjoyable, and spirited programme environment.

THE CASE FOR CHANGE

Your Notes/Questions:

Key Points	Your Questions/Comments
• _____	_____
• _____	_____
• _____	_____
• _____	_____
• _____	_____
• _____	_____
• _____	_____
• _____	_____

CASE FOR CHANGE—YOUR TEAM'S QUESTIONS

After discussion of the Case for Change presentation in your team, agree on and list the priority questions that your team would like to raise.

1. _____
2. _____
3. _____
4. _____
5. _____

FORCES FOR CHANGE: ORGANISATIONAL COMMITMENTS

During your team's discussion of organisational commitments met, in progress, or planned, use the following chart to note the specifics of those that are of particular interest to you and those with whom you work.

What Is Underway or Planned	Why?	Time Frame?
_____		
_____		
_____		
_____		
_____		
_____		

MY PERSONAL CHALLENGE

My Behaviour

What can I start doing, stop doing, or do more of to help my company succeed?

Others' Behaviour

How can I positively influence others to help our company succeed?

My Boss's Behaviour

What helpful advice, feedback, and support can I give my boss?

TEAM IDEAS

On conclusion of your team's discussion of ideas that might help the company better meet the business challenges discussed today and achieve desired results as a company, agree as a team and provide *one* suggestion, idea, or improvement for consideration by senior management. Fill in the information below.

Specific Problem/Issue/Opportunity Addressed:

Your Team's Idea to Solve the Problem or Improve the Situation:

Benefits of Implementing Your Team's Idea:

Changes Required to Make Your Idea a Reality:

FEEDBACK ON THE PROGRAMME

Fill out the information below:

Value/helpfulness of today's program
to you

1 2 3 4 5 6 7 8 9 10
Very Low   Very High

Value/helpfulness of today's program
to the company

1 2 3 4 5 6 7 8 9 10
Very Low   Very High

Your comments on the programme:

Advice to the CEO and Executive Committee:

Will you commit to the personal challenge that you have identified today? Will you take action? (circle one)

Yes   No

Name/Contact Number (optional):

Glossary

Adaptive—The ability of an organization to change how it operates based on objective external data.

Alignment—Getting a common focus across the organization in terms of organizational intent, daily behavior, processes and procedures, and results.

Analysis—Looking at data and arriving at conclusions as to what the data means for the organization.

Attributional Models—Cultural survey forms, usually off the shelf, that purport to measure the organization against some predetermined value system or set of attributes.

Behavioral Practices—The patterns of behavior intended to produce a particular result.

Brand—A direct or indirect promise to the customer about what to expect from a given company or product.

Corporate Culture—Patterns of behavior that are overtly or covertly agreed by a group as the proper way to behave in any given situation.

CDD—Cultural Due Diligence.

Cross-Border Merger—A merger of two or more businesses where some parts of the combining businesses reside in different countries.

Constituencies—Groups of people to whom a manager or company needs to be responsive in order to achieve the management or organizational purpose.

Consequences—The personal impact on an individual as a result of his or her behavior.

Continuum—A range of possible activity or response to anything.

Culture Clash—The disagreements that occur when two or more groups of people have different views as to what behavior or action is appropriate in any given situation.

Cultural Compatibility—The degree to which the cultures of two organizations, while different, are not in conflict and tend to support one another.

Cultural Triage—The activity of a consultant when intervening in culture clash; a quick assessment of which parts of a culture clash need to be dealt with first; priority setting for intervention into culture clash.

Declarative Change—An organizational change that is required and little discussion about the nature of the change is allowable.

Demographic Data—Background data on any particular group, such as age, educational background, tenure, and so forth.

Diagnostic—An analysis of a business situation intended to indicate appropriate actions in response to the situation.

Divestiture—Selling off a part of a company.

Domains—Categories of data; groupings of data into particular "buckets" to aid in understanding it.

Due Diligence—The required activity of responsible parties to assure that their actions, undertaken for the benefit of others, are not irresponsible nor negligent.

Empirical—Objective data not colored by personal opinion.

Empowered—Given the power to make decisions and take action.

Executive Team—The most senior team in any particular organizational unit or the most senior team in the organization, usually composed of the corporate officers.

Exemplary—An example of how something is properly done.

External Environment—Factors outside of the organization that have an impact on the organization.

Facilitation—Helping individuals or groups interact with activities or questions without taking a direct part in the discussion or activity yourself.

Focus Groups—A group of seven to twelve people from whom data is collected on a specific business topic or topics.

Globalization—The movement of commerce beyond the boundaries of any particular country.

Golden Handcuffs—An agreement, usually with executives or key employees, to pay a specified bonus if they stay with a company for a certain period of time.

Granularity—The degree of detail of data; the greater the granularity the finer the detail.

HR—Human Resources.

Homogeneity—Composed of similar or identical elements.

Incremental Change—A series of small changes over time.

Indirect Costs—Costs of an activity that are not directly tied to cash, such as the cost of a meeting, expressed as the sum of the average salary cost per minute of each person in the meeting.

Infrastructure—The organization, policies and procedures, and systems of an organization.

Integration—Taking two or more units or processes and combining them into one activity or group.

Interdependent—Two or more units or activities that depend on one another to be successful.

IPO—Taking part of an organization, or a privately held organization, and turning it into an independent, publicly held company.

IT—Information Technology. The term may be applied to the systems or to the department that runs the systems.

Leadership—The actions of individuals that directly influence the behavior and attitudes of others.

Letter of Intent/Acceptance—A formal and legally binding announcement of an intent of one company to acquire another. (Acceptance is a UK term and intent is a U.S. term.)

Leverage—Utilizing things that are working reasonably well in additional areas to increase those results.

Line Systems—Operational systems that are employed in the manufacture and production of a company's products and services.

Malfeasance—Wrongdoing or misconduct on the part of a person who has legal responsibility for acting appropriately in the given situation.

Management—Planning, directing, staffing, and controlling work.

Matrix Management—A management structure in which people have both functional and project responsibilities and report simultaneously to two or more people.

Morale—The general mental state of the employees of any organization, generally referring to their feelings of trust, confidence, enthusiasm, and willingness.

Morphed—Something that has over time changed into something else.

Negligence—Not taking actions that a knowledgeable and prudent person would have taken; ignoring responsibility.

Organizational Alignment—Assuring that the organizational strategy, organizational culture, and organizational infrastructure are coordinated and support each other.

Organizational Culture—Patterns of behavior that are overtly or covertly agreed by a group as the proper way to behave in any given situation.

Organizational Performance—The results of daily organizational activity.

Organizational Practices—The behavioral norms in going about the daily business of an organization.

Organizational Scan—The activity of analyzing the overall performance of an organizational system.

Participative Change—An organizational change in which the people impacted by the change have an opportunity to provide input into the nature and manner of the impending change.

Performance Specifications—The specified quantity and quality levels of any particular task or activity.

Premium—An amount of money paid by the acquiring company that exceeds the empirically derived value of the company being acquired.

Productivity—Overall output of the company or of the employees of the organization.

Quality Initiatives—Special projects, usually transformational in nature, intended to impact and improve the quality of the goods or services produced.

Qualitative—Having to do with the quality or qualities of something rather than with the quantity.

Quantitative—How many or how often; a measure of frequency or amount.

Re-Engineering—The redesign of how something is done or how a process is carried out.

Silo Effect—The tendency of individual units or functions in an organization to become solely focused on their particular part of the organization to the exclusion of concern or care about other areas of the company.

Stakeholders—People or groups that have a vested interest in the health and success of a company; the shareholders, employees, customers, suppliers, and community in which the company operates.

Staff Functions—Activities of the organization that support the overall organization's purpose but are not directly involved in the production or delivery of the services/products that the company exists to produce; examples are HR and Legal Departments.

Strategic Alliance—An agreement between two organizations to work together and support each other in some specified activity to achieve mutual gain.

Subculture—A set of behavioral standards/patterns unique to a particular part of the organization that are not characteristic of the entire organization.

Synergy—The phenomena of increasing efficiency in any particular activity through a combining of previously separate activities.

Synthesis—An understanding of how all the various parts of a system combine to produce any given result.

System—A number of separate units or parts working interdependently to produce a given product or service.

System Theory—A known and applicable body of knowledge and practice derived from working with organizational systems.

Systematic—Made or arranged according to a system, method, or plan.

Systemic—Of or affecting the entire organization or system.

Target Company—The company that another company wants to buy in a merger or acquisition.

Transform—To change the condition, nature, or function of an organization.

Transformation—The activity of transforming an organization.

Transformational Change—A major change in the way a company operates affecting all or most of the organization; not incremental change.

Transplantation—Taking something from one organization or area and applying it in another organization or area.

Value-Based Difference—A difference in behaving that people interpret as having meaning beyond the specifics of the behavior itself; that is, people who act that way must believe . . . .

Values—An important belief or principle that acts as a guide for daily behavior, actions, and decisions.

Variables—The various things that may have a bearing on why something is happening.

Vision—A statement to make clear the intent or ultimate purpose of an organization in sufficient detail to provide definitive guidance for action.

References

Andrade, G., Mitchell, M., & Stafford, E. (AMS) (2001). New evidence and perspectives on mergers, *Journal of Economic Perspectives, 15*(2), pp. 103–120.

Anders, G. (2003). *Perfect enough: Carly Fiorina and the reinvention of Hewlett Packard.* New York: Penguin Group.

Ackoff, R. L. (1999). *Ackoff's best.* New York: John Wiley & Sons.

Beckham, J. D. (1995, September/October). Altered states. *Healthcare Forum Journal.*

Bohl, D. L. (1989). *Tying the corporate knot: An American Management Association research report on the effects of mergers and acquisitions.* Washington, DC: American Management Association.

Burke, W. W., & Litwin, G. H. (1989). "A model of organizational change and performance." In J. W. Pfeiffer (Ed.), 1989 Annual: *Developing Human Resources* (pp. 277–288). San Francisco: Pfeiffer.

Buono, A. F., & Bowditch, J. L. (1989). *The human side of mergers and acquisitions.* San Francisco: Jossey-Bass.

Buono, A. F., & Nurick, A. J. (2001). Intervening in the middle: Coping strategies in mergers and acquisitions. *Human Resource Planning, 15*(2).

Carleton, J. R. (1997, November). Cultural due diligence: A concept long overdue. *Training,* pp. 67–75.

Carleton, J. R. (2001). *Due diligence: Law and practice: Cultural due diligence.* London: Maxwell & Sweet.

Carleton, J. R., & Lineberry, C. S. (1992). Culture change. In H. D. Stolovitch & E. J. Keeps (Eds.), *Handbook of human performance technology.* San Francisco: Jossey-Bass.

Carleton, J. R., & Tosti, D. (1979). "Productivity improvement." San Rafael, CA: Operants Inc.

Cartwright, S., & Cooper, C. L. (1996). *Managing mergers, acquisitions and strategic alliances: Integrating people and cultures.* London: Butterworth-Heinemann.

Cartwright, S., & Cooper, C. L. (1995). Organizational marriage: "Hard" versus "soft" issues. *Personnel Review, 24*(3).

Clemente, M. N., & Greenspan, D. S. (1998). *Winning at mergers and acquisitions: The guide to market-focused planning and integration.* New York: John Wiley & Sons.

Craig, G. R., & Lineberry, C. (2001). Management mirror: Helping senior management teams see their own reality. *Industrial and Commercial Training, 33.* West Yorkshire, UK: MCB University Press.

Deal, T., & Kennedy, A. (1982). *Corporate cultures: The rites and rituals of corporate life.* New York: Addison-Wesley.

Fahey, A., & Goldman, D. (1994, October 3). The fall and rise of DDB. *Ad Week, 16*(40).

Fairfield, K. D. (1992, May). 10 myths of managing a merger. *Across the Board, 29*(5).

Feldman, M. L. (1995, July/August). Disaster prevention plans after a merger. *Mergers & Acquisitions, 30*(1).

Fiduciary relations in corporate law. (1991). *Canadian Business Law Journal, 19,* pp. 1–27.

Galpin, T. J., & Herndon, M. (2000). *The complete guide to mergers and acquisitions: Process tools to support M&A integration at every level.* San Francisco: Jossey-Bass.

Giving diligence its due. (1995, February). *Management Today.*

Goldberg, W. H. (1983). *Mergers: Motives, modes, methods.* London: Nichols Press.

Harbig, A. J. (1994). Culture: The hidden dimension in international mergers and acquisitions. *SIETAR EUROPA.*

Harvey, M. G., & Lusch, R. F. (1995, January). Expanding the nature and scope of due diligence. *Journal of Business Venturing, 10*(1).

Healy, P. M., Palepu, K. G., & Ruback, R. S. (1992). Does corporate performance improve after mergers? *Journal of Financial Economics, 31.*

Hofstede, G. (1980). *Culture's consequences.*

Hofstede, G. (1991). *Cultures and organizations: Software of the mind.* New York: McGraw-Hill.

Homans, G. C. (1950). *The human group.* New York: Harcourt Brace.

House, R. (1994, May). Cross-border alliances: What works, what doesn't. *Institutional Investor, 28*(5).

Hubbard, G., Lofstrom, S., & Tulley, R. (1994, September). Diligence checklists: Do they get the best answers? *Mergers & Acquisitions, 29*(2).

Ireland, K. (1991, November). Mastering a foreign acquisition. *Personnel Journal, 70*(11).

Key, S. L. (Ed.). (1989). *The Ernst & Young management guide to mergers and acquisitions.* New York: John Wiley & Sons. [Especially see "Culture," Chapter 16, pp. 229–243.]

Klein, A. (2003). Stealing time: Steve Case, Jerry Levin and the collapse of AOL Time Warner. New York: Simon & Schuster.

Kotter, J. P., & Heskett, J. L. (1992). *Corporate culture and performance.* New York: The Free Press.

Kransdorff, A. (1993, May). Making acquisitions work by the book. *Personnel Management, 25*(5).

Lajoux, A. R. (1998). *The art of M & A integration: A guide to merging resources, processes, and responsibilities.* New York: McGraw-Hill.

Langdon, D. G. (2000). *Aligning performance: Improving people, systems and organizations.* San Francisco: Pfeiffer.

Lineberry, C. S., & Carleton, J. R. (1992). Organizational culture change. In *Handbook of human performance technology* (Vol. 1). San Francisco: Jossey-Bass.

Lineberry, C. S., & Carleton, J. R. (1999). Analyzing corporate culture. In *Handbook of human performance technology* (Vol. 2). San Francisco: Jossey-Bass.

Marks, M. L., & Mirvis, P. H. (1992, April). Tracking the impact of mergers and acquisitions. *Personnel Journal, 71*(4).

McGlickin, R., & Nuyen, S. (1995). On productivity and plant ownership change: New evidence from the longitudinal research data base. *Rand Journal of Economics, 26*, pp. 257–276.

McNair, J. (1994, May 15). *Merger failures costing shareholders billions.* San Jose, CA: Knight-Ridder/Tribune Business News.

Medina-Walker, D., Walker, T., & Schmitz, J. (2002). *Doing business internationally: The guide to cross-cultural success* (2nd ed.). New York: McGraw-Hill.

Merging corporate cultures. (1994, May 5). *Hospitals & Health Networks, 68*(9).

Montague, J. (1995, February 5). When the smoke clears. *Hospitals & Health Networks, 69*(3).

Mitchell, M. L., & Lane, K. (1990). Do bad bidders become good targets? *Journal of Political Economy, 98*, pp. 372–398.

Mueller, D. C. (1986). *Profits in the long run.* New York: Cambridge University Press.

Ouchi, W. G. (1981). *Theory Z: How American business can meet the Japanese challenge.* Boulder, CO: Perseus Publishing.

Pascale, R. T., & Athos, A. G. (1981). *The art of Japanese management:* Applications for American executive. New York: Warner Books.

O'Toole, J. (1985). *Vanguard management: Redesigning the corporate future.* Garden City, NY: Doubleday.

Pimentel, B. (2003, May 4). New HP delivers, but doubts remain. *Wall Street Journal.*

Post-merger: Dealing with that "corporate culture thing. (1994, June). *Trustee, 7*(6).

Raab, D., & Clark, A. E. (1992, May). Mindful management for merger mania. *Bankers Monthly, CIX*(5).

Raunuyar, R. (2003, March 24). Fiorina on reinventing Hewlett Packard, self. *Wharton Journal.*

Reed, S. F., & Lajoux, A. R. (1995). *The art of M & A—A merger acquisition buyout guide* (2nd ed.). Burr Ridge, IL: Irwin Professional Publishing.

Reynolds, P. C. (1987, March 1987). Imposing a corporate culture. *Psychology Today,* pp. 33–38.

Rhinesmith, S. (1996). *A manager's guide to globalization: Six keys to success in a changing world.* New York: McGraw-Hill.

Ritti, R. R., & Funkhouser, G. R. (1982). *Ropes to skip and the ropes to know.* New York: John Wiley & Sons, Inc.

Rowlinson, M. (1995, March). The strategy, structure and culture: Cadbury, divisionalization and merger in the 1960s. *Journal of Management Studies, 32*(2).

Rummler, G., & Brache, A. P. (1992). *Improving performance: How to manage the white space on the organizational chart.* San Francisco: Jossey-Bass.

Schein, E. (1968). *Process consultation: Its role in organization development.* Reading, MA: Addison Wesley Publishing Company.

Schein, E. (1978). *Career dynamics: Matching individual and organizational needs.* Reading, MA: Addison Wesley Publishing Company.

Schein, E. (1995). *Strategic pragmatism: The culture of Singapore's economic development board.* Cambridge: The MIT Press.

Schenk, H. (2000a). *Mergers, efficient choice and international competitiveness.* Cheltenham, England: Edward Elgar.

Schenk, H. (2000b). Are international acquisitions a matter of strategy rather than wealth creation? *International Review of Applied Economics.*

Schoar, A. (2002). New evidence and perspectives on mergers. *Journal of Finance, 57*(6), pp. 2379–2403.

Sirower, M. (1997). *The synergy trap.*

Stern, S. (1994, April). The odd couples. *International Management, 49*(3).

Taguiri, R., & Litwin, G. H. (1968). *Organizational climate: Exploration of a concept. Boston.*

Tosti, D. T., & Jackson, S. (1994, April). Alignment: How it works and why it matters. *Training.*

Trompenaars, F. (1997). *Riding the waves of culture: Understanding cultural diversity in business.* London: Nicholas Brealey.

Van Maanen, J. (1976). *Organizational careers: Some new perspectives.* New York: John Wiley & Sons, Inc.

Van Maanen, J. (1979). *Demographics & destiny.* New York: John Wiley & Sons, Inc.

Watson Wyatt (1999). The war for talent.

Zweig, P. L. (1995, January 16). Tense scenes from a marriage. *Business Week.*

Zweig, P. L. (1995, October 30). The case against mergers. *Business Week,* pp. 122–130.

Index

M

M&A failures: costs of, 9–13; culture clash as cause of, 13–14, 17; increasing concern of stakeholders regarding, 1–2; report card on, 8–9

M&A failures costs: bad bidders become good targets, 10; brand confusion, 12; changes in productivity, 10; decreased customer service levels/satisfaction, 12–13; decreased profitability, 10; excessive acquisition premiums, 9–10; lack of external focus on customer, competition, marketplace, 10–11; loss of key executives, 11; loss of key staff, 11–12; low staff motivation/morale, 11; lower of market share, 10; lower share price, 9

M&A (mergers and acquisitions): creation of successful, 121–122; cultural integration success measures, 118–119; financial success measures of, 117–118; increasing rate of, 7–8; pre letter of intent/acceptance activities, 61–63; success of Hewlett Packard-Compaq, 65–67; typical post-merger performance, 14*fig*

McGlickin, R., 10

McKinsey Consulting study, 9

McNealy, S., 66

Management: aligning, 99–110; daily behavior as driver of culture, 32; multicultural team leadership in, 21–22; system-aware and system-sensitive, 24; systems and, 29–30. *See also* CEO; Change management; Executive group

Management action plans, 114

Manager's Action Planning Guide, 107

A Manager's Guide to Globalization (Rhinesmith), 20

Medina-Walker, D., 22

Mercedes-Benz, 20

Mitchell, M. L., 9, 10

Mueller, D. C., 10

Multicultural team leadership: "American" profile of, 22; characteristics of, 21; considering local culture in selecting, 22

N

National culture, 20–22

Nations Bank, 12

Nguyen, S., 10

Nissan, 20

O

Organizational alignment: described, 35–36; systemic approach to, 36–37. *See also* Cultural alignment

Organizational Alignment Model: capstone for, 97*fig*; illustrated diagram of, 36*fig*; on three interdependent drivers of results, 37

Organizational culture: adaptive vs. non-adaptive, 20; British Airways case study in managing, 16; culture clash and, 15–16; debate over, 17; defining, 18–19; hard data on performance and, 19–20; management daily behavior as driver of, 32; misinformation on, 16–17; national vs., 20–22; as separate from systems, 31–33. *See also* Culture

Organizational Scan process, 35

Organizational System Model: described, 37–38; external focus of, 38–39*fig*; organizational focus of, 38*fig*

Organizational System Scan Model: organizational level of, 44*fig*–46; overview of, 39–40*fig*, 41; overview of the, 46–47; people level of, 43*fig*–44; Values

W

Walker, T., 22

The Wall Street Journal, 21

Watson-Wyatt, 13

Watson-Wyatt study (1999), 14

Wharton Journal News, 66

Work processes: CDD identification of, 73; re-engineering, 115*fig*–116

X

Xerox, 20

About the Authors

J. Robert Carleton, is co-founder, CEO and a senior partner of Vector Group, Inc., and a director of Vector Europe, Ltd. He has worked in both the public and private sectors and has extensive experience as both a manager and consultant. During his tenure as manager of research and evaluation and director of executive development for Southland Corporation, he served as internal executive coach to the members of the senior management team. Carleton also served as director of training and organization development for Alameda County, California.

As a consultant, he has delivered measurable results while implementing significant organizational change. His clients include Hewlett-Packard, Compaq, British Airways Cargo, General Motors, Groupe Schneider, and W.R. Grace. He has developed and published seminal articles on the concept of cultural due diligence in increasing success in mergers, acquisitions, and alliances. He co-authored, with Claude Lineberry, the chapters on organizational culture change and analysis of corporate culture for the *Handbook of Human Performance Technology,* Volumes 1 and 2 (Jossey-Bass 1992, 1999). Carleton is a past president and founding director of the International Board of Standards for Training, Performance, and Instruction and a frequent presenter and featured speaker at international conferences.

He can be reached at the Vector Group, Inc., offices in Conifer, Colorado, (303) 838-1048, or by email at jrc@vectorscan.com. The Vector Group website is www.vector.org.

Claude S. Lineberry is co-founder, COO and a senior partner of Vector Group, Inc., and a director of Vector Europe, Ltd. He has worked on a wide range of organizational issues with a variety of clients over the last thirty years, ranging from increasing manufacturing productivity to improving customer service. His clients include Hewlett-Packard, Compaq, British Airways Cargo, W.R. Grace, Prudential Financial Services—UK, and Merck.

He has extensive experience in the development and delivery of 360-degree-based leadership programs and executive coaching, having served as a coach to senior executives at British Airways, Merck, PricewaterhouseCoopers, and National Westminster Bank. Lineberry is co-author with Bob Carleton of the chapters on Organizational Culture Change and Analyzing Corporate Culture in the *Handbook of Human Performance Technology,* Volumes 1 and 2 (Jossey-Bass, 1992, 1999). Lineberry is a past president of the International Society of Performance Improvement and was recently made an Honorary Life Member in recognition of his long-term contribution to the field of organizational effectiveness. He is a frequent speaker at international conferences and the author of numerous journal articles. He holds a B.A. from the University of Alabama and an M.A. from the University of Connecticut and has done additional doctoral-level graduate work at the Catholic University of America.

The Vector Group website is www.vector.org

On December 2, 2003 in Oakland, California, Claude had an adverse reaction to a drug given at the conclusion of what would have been a successful operation. Much loved as a father and husband, he was much loved and admired as a mentor, coach, and advisor to many who knew him.

Farewell my friend, we could never have gotten so far so fast without you.

Bob Carleton – December 15, 2003

How to Use the CD-ROM

SYSTEM REQUIREMENTS

Windows PC

- 486 or Pentium processor-based personal computer
- Microsoft Windows 95 or Windows NT 3.51 or later
- Minimum RAM: 8MB for Windows 95 and NT
- Available space on hard disk: 8 MB Windows 95 and NT
- 2X speed CD-ROM drive or faster

Macintosh

- Macintosh with a 68020 or higher processor or Power Macintosh
- Apple OS version 7.0 or later
- Minimum RAM: 12MB for Macintosh
- Available space on hard disk: 6MB Macintosh
- 2X speed CD-ROM drive or faster

NOTE: This CD-ROM requires Netscape 3.0 or MS Internet Explorer 3.0 or higher. You can download these products using the links on the CD-ROM Help Page.

GETTING STARTED

Insert the CD-ROM into your drive. The CD-ROM will usually launch automatically. If it does not, click on the CD-ROM drive on your computer to launch. After you click to agree to the terms of the Copyright Page, the Home Page will appear.

MOVING AROUND

Use the buttons at the left of each screen to move among the menu pages. To view a document listed on one of the menu pages, simply click on the name of the document. To quit a document at any time, click the box at the upper right-hand corner of the screen.

To quit the CD-ROM, you can click the Exit button or hit Alt-F4.

TO DOWNLOAD DOCUMENTS

Open the document you wish to download. Under the File pulldown menu, choose Save As. Save the document onto your hard drive with a different name. It is important to use a different name, otherwise the document may remain a read-only file.

You can also click on your CD drive in Windows Explorer and select a document to copy to your hard drive and rename it.

IN CASE OF TROUBLE

If you experience difficulty using this CD-ROM, please follow these steps:

1. Make sure your hardware and systems configurations conform to the systems requirements noted under "Systems Requirements" above.

2. Review the installation procedure for your type of hardware and operating system. It is possible to reinstall the software if necessary.

3. Have a question, comment, or suggestion? Contact us! We value your feedback, and we want to hear from you.

For questions about this or other Pfeiffer products, you may contact us by:

E-mail: customer@wiley.com
Mail: Customer Care Wiley/Pfeiffer
          10475 Crosspoint Blvd.
          Indianapolis, IN 46256
Phone: (U.S.) 800-274-4434 (Outside the U.S. 317-572-3985)
Fax: (U.S.) 800-569-0443 (Outside the U.S. 317-572-4002)

To order additional copies of this product or to browse other Pfeiffer products, visit us online at www.pfeiffer.com.

To speak with someone in Product Technical Support, call 800-762-2974 or 317-572-3994 Monday through Friday 8:30 a.m. to 5 p.m. (EST). You can also contact Product Technical Support and get support information through our website at http://www.wiley.com/techsupport

Before calling or writing, please have the following information available:

- Type of operating system
- Any error messages displayed
- Complete description of the problem

It is best if you are sitting at your computer when making the call.